Personal Peace

Transcending Your Interpersonal Limits

Robert L. McKinley, M.D.

New Harbinger Publications, Inc.
5674 Shattuck Avenue
Oakland, CA 94609

To Mary

Contents

Preface

I want to give you a gift of personal peace. I want to help you escape the habits that stand between you and personal peace. Perhaps this seems a formidable undertaking, but in fact the task proceeds quite simply and logically. I will lead you along a path to personal peace which is straightforward and sure.

To give you the gift of personal peace, I must teach you many things. I ask you to trust me and to allow me to teach you these things. At the end you will grasp how all these teachings fit together. These teachings will enable you to lay hold of a personal peace which will never more escape you.

This book will help you see and manage your interpersonal relationships. You could hardly undertake a more ambitious project. Interpersonal interactions surround us from birth to death, like the sea surrounds its fishes. These interactions continually present themselves for our inspection and study. Without learning to see and study, you will not become familiar with the events in your interpersonal environment. This book will show you what to look for and help you to master the events of your own interpersonal world.

What does mastery of your interpersonal environment have to do with lasting personal peace? With just a little instruction, I can enable you to find and grasp your personal peace. But I must teach you much more to enable you to recognize all the continual temptations to abandon your peace. I must make you familiar with your interpersonal habit, those ways you habitually use to manage your relations with others. *Your interpersonal habit continually tempts you to throw away your personal peace.* Interpersonal habit promises that you can make others do as you please by throwing away your personal peace.

Mastery of your interpersonal world will enable you to spot and avoid these temptations to throw away your peace. Only thus can you abandon the habit of throwing away your peace to try to make others do as you wish. This explains why I need a whole book, and not just a few paragraphs, to give you this gift.

This study of the interpersonal environment has broad application. This book could as well serve as a resource in the study of language, belief systems, culture, or management. These and many other fields consist of sets of interpersonal operations and depend on interpersonal skills for their practice.

You won't find what this book invites you to look for in this book. The book will show you *where* to look. Once you see the events that the book points to, you can throw the book away. This is so whenever a book deals with tangible, experiential things. No one can put the smell of an apple into words. No one can put the touch of a hand into words. A book can tell you where to seek the smell of an apple. A book can tell you how to arrange for the touch of a hand. My book can tell you where and how to look to discover personal peace. My book can tell you where and how to look for temptation to abandon your peace. Once you have found personal peace you must learn not to fall to temptation to abandon that peace. Then you will always have this gift.

As you read, you will notice that I sometimes use words in new and unusual ways. New ways of looking require new ways of using words and different structures of language. Words and language arise as interpersonal tools. The tool must fit the job, and so words, language, and the structure of language arise as ways to manage others. Words, language, and language structure arise as ways to practice interpersonal habit. So interpersonal habit determines the words, language and language structure.

Our talk serves our interpersonal habit, and so *we say whatever works*. You can see how this arrangement can get tricky for those who do not see the underlying interpersonal habit.

When we rely on words to point out *never before seen events*, we embark on an enterprise which requires care. I must take care that my words do not lead you astray. I try to use the lowest level of abstraction that will do the job. I try to make the words I use stand clearly for things.

Usually we fill up our talk with many nonreferential words, hoping such words will affect the other as we wish. We may not realize that many of our words do not stand for anything to those with whom we talk. We merely engage in social chanting with such talk. I like socializing and I like chanting, but if I am to tell you how and where to look for something I must use referential words. Directing a search demands words of the lowest abstraction, words that stand for something to the listener.

I talk considerably about child development. I consider this approach essential. *Ordinary children develop a complete system for managing other people before they reach four and one-half years of age.* Children learn a set of ways to manage other people before they can make their words stand for things.

This people-managing system that the five-year-old child has mastered *depends chiefly upon the child's throwing away his personal peace.* He manages others with his crying or discontenting. Crying, suffering, and discontenting to get others to perform so completely engages him that *he pays no attention to his state of peace.*

You and I developed our own system for managing other people before we reached the age of five years. Until we learn better, we will practice this same system on and on. I want to give you the gift of escaping from this infant-child system. I want to give you the gift of escape from falling prey to the temptation of abandoning peace as the infant does. I want to give you the gift of escaping the habit of abandoning peace to affect others.

This is why I dwell on the child and his parents. If you cannot see how a four-year-old operates, you cannot see how you and I operate. If you cannot see what parents and children do with each other, then you cannot see what adults do with each other. You cannot see adults throw away their personal peace as a negotiation.

To see what my book pictures, you must watch what you do with others and what they do with you. This unfamiliar practice may frighten, awe, or dismay you at first. Further practice will lead to assurance, adventure, and even delight. Making the first hurdle takes courage. I want you to take that frightening leap.

In the movie *Treasure of Sierra Madre*, the old prospector begins to dance a jig. His two companions think he has lost his sanity. He calls them "dumb donkeys" and continues to whoop and yell and dance. *He knows how to see and sees gold!* They don't know how to see and see nothing. I want to teach you how to see the continual negotiations between you and others.

My anecdotes share real people with you to help you *to begin to examine what people do with each other*. I have changed the names and the circumstances to conceal their identities.

1

Bewildered

Tom and Nancy walk into my office looking young, intelligent, and attractive. They look like the kind of couple that I would wish to have as nextdoor neighbors. They look like a couple with whom I would wish to make friends.

Tom and Nancy complain that unhappiness has overshadowed them. After five years of marriage, they have fallen into a pattern of frequent discord. They regularly assault each other with vicious words. These clashes intensely distress them both. They seek help because they cannot understand or resolve their controversy.

I begin to gather facts about their relationship.

Their clashes start in a set pattern. Tom begins some affectionate approach. Nancy then complains of fatigue, or a headache. She complains that the daily grind has drained her. Tom grows angry and vows that he will take a lover unless something changes. Nancy begins her own angry counterattack with vicious words, but the threat of abandonment soon brings her to tears and panic. She begs and whines and despairs while Tom insists that Nancy had better change. After a couple of days the storm abates and both dejectedly go about their vocational activities.

Tom and Nancy do enjoy moments of affection, and occasionally enjoy sexual pleasure together. Nevertheless, the quarrelsome pattern consumes more and more of their time together. They can quarrel and fight but *they cannot talk about what they do with each other.*

In counseling, Nancy's aim is to preserve the marriage. She admits wanting to appear sexually attractive. She finds men at school attractive but states that at home she feels sexually unwelcome. Tom finds Nancy's view hard to believe. He views himself as always ready to make love. Tom's aim is to help Nancy overcome her problem with closeness. He thinks that Nancy sees herself as a bad person and untouchable. He sees this as the problem, a problem that he cannot solve.

They are both quite capable of articulating these explanations of their situation. However, their explanations do nothing to resolve their conflict or mitigate their dismay. *How can two intelligent capable adults remain so unclear about their interpersonal relationship?*

I ask them about their history together. What attracted Tom to Nancy and Nancy to Tom?

They tell me that they found each other when both were students in pre-law school. Intuitively drawn together, they started to cling to each other. Soon they decided to live together. Later they married.

During those school years, they lived with poverty, overwork, fatigue, and general self-neglect. They endured these difficulties to achieve graduation.

From what they tell me of that life arrangement, I see that Tom assumed a parental role with Nancy. He worked hard at supporting and comforting Nancy. Nancy assumed a child role with Tom. She acted helpless, apprehensive, and insecure. They have maintained this union of the helpless waif and the caring parent throughout their professional training. And now that the end of their training is approaching, they have begun to quarrel with increasing frequency.

Soon Tom will assume a professional and adult role. Nancy will also assume a professional role, one that she is undeniably adequate to perform. Both will spend most of their day working at their profession. Prosperity approaches. Something about that prospect unsettles them.

Both will lose the old familiar world of hardships and ordeals. They will lose the arrangement on which they have depended for so long for their sense of orientation.

How did Tom learn to play his parental role? How did Nancy learn to play the role of helpless waif? And what do these roles do for them? *What is it that they are negotiating for from each other?*

In early childhood Tom learned that he could keep his waiflike mother pleased and calm by taking a parental role with her. In his habitual role as parent, Tom cannot admit that Nancy is an adequate adult. Tom has an investment in the waif image of Nancy. He knows what to do with a waif. The image of Nancy as a woman threatens Tom with the possibility of abandonment. (His threats to find someone else suggest that he feels threatened.) If he cannot play the parent, he can play the angering, "I'm going to get me another mommy" child.

Nancy has depended all her life on playing the helpless waif. That role has succeeded in wooing comfort and support from her significant others. But the imminent exposure of her womanhood threatens to strip away the waif mask she wears. With her waif role exposed, she knows no other dependable way to negotiate for presence and nurture from the other. So she resorts to angering and quarreling. (This alternative strategy suggests that she was able to garner some support from others in the past with this negotiation.)

When their ordeal-world goes, also go the settings that have ratified the roles of supportive parent and helpless waif. Tom and Nancy suffer at the prospect of adulthood. Their long-accustomed way of relating is crumbling fast. They face new and unfamiliar roles, and these new roles threaten them.

Meanwhile the fighting provides a reprieve, a slowed pace into the new world. Fighting diverts their focus away from the crumbling basis for their customary roles with each other. A good fight also involves plenty of physical closeness. A fight dramatically displays the other's presence, and provides relief from the sense of impending unknown.

Tom and Nancy will make it. With counseling, they will move into a new adulthood. They will find peace and joy in new ways of relating. They will learn to transcend the parent-child contract in which they began their lives together.

What about the questions we asked about Tom and Nancy's interpersonal world? Have we answered them?

What attracted Tom to Nancy and Nancy to Tom? How did they learn to play their roles? What is it that they are negotiating for from each other? And how can two intelligent capable adults remain so unclear about their interpersonal world?

I want to teach you to read. I want to teach you to read people. Specifically, I want to teach you to read what people do with each other in seeking to fulfill their wishes.

I call what people do with each other *interpersonal operations.* For example, I am now operating with you, bidding with you, or negotiating with you. I negotiate for your attention and to get you to stay with me through my book. When I speak of two people working with each other to fulfill their wishes, I call what they do *negotiating* or *operating.*

A Harvard professor, B.F. Skinner, first used the term *operation* as a way of studying animal behavior. Armed with this term, he devised and conducted many experiments with animals. From his work, a new, clear, and impressive body of knowledge about animal behavior emerged. Most significantly, he gave us a new way of understanding how animals gain new behaviors. In other words, he showed us how animals *learn.* (By implication, he also showed us how to *teach.*)

Skinner called the nucleus of his experimental findings *operant conditioning.* Part of this map of animal learning says that certain events following a behavior increase the animal's repetition of that behavior. For example, giving a morsel of food to a pigeon immediately after the pigeon stretches its neck teaches the bird to stretch its neck more frequently. After a few such feedings, the pigeon vigorously and frequently stretches it neck. Skinner called those events that increase behavior *reinforcers*.

Thanks to Skinner, we have practical maps about animal learning. We know about the acquisition of persistent behaviors by animals. *These maps apply to us human animals as well.*

We humans do simple operations on objects to derive their length or weight or texture. *Much more significantly, we do operations on each other.* You and I can watch and learn to see these operations.

I want to each you to read. I want to teach you to see interpersonal operations—that is, to see the negotiations that make up *our interpersonal world.* The interpersonal world surrounds us like the sea surrounds the fish. Do the fish see the sea? Humans don't see the interpersonal world until they experience something that opens their eyes. I want my book to give you that experience.

When we see the interpersonal matrix around us, we pierce the veil of our illusions. Behind that veil, we perceive the mysteries hidden from the beginning in what humans like Tom and Nancy and you and I do with each other.

I ask you to make an agreement with me. I want you to make the one assumption that *anytime two humans meet, they continually operate with each other.* Put another way, they continually negotiate with each other. If you will entertain that one assumption, I will teach you to read people. Fair enough?

We can begin here and now to learn the main skill you'll need in order to see the hidden interpersonal world. That skill is simply *knowing how to get yourself into the here and now.* Begin to focus your attention right here and right now, with no self-talk and no thinking, just watching and listening, as you take your first step toward seeing yourself in your interpersonal world.

Do this exercise for me. Find a piece of paper and

something to write with and copy down these words:

> *I am not hungry. I am not thirsty. I am not too hot.*
> *I am not too cold. I am not in pain. I am not being*
> *attacked.*

Now repeat these words to yourself. Tell yourself, "I am not hungry. I am not thirsty. I am not too hot. I am not too cold. I am not in pain. I am not being attacked."

Please pay absolute attention to what you are telling yourself. If any of these statements is not true, leave off the exercise and go correct the situation. Have something to eat, or turn up the thermostat. If you feel a tangible pain, such as a toothache or the pain of a gashed finger, attend to it. Then come back to the exercise.

When you say these words, you are describing your here and now as a state of peace and comfort. You live here and now in a state of peace and comfort. *You already have personal peace.*

Once you grasp that your true state is peace and comfort, you can begin to watch what you do with this state. You can begin to see the moments when you hold onto your peace and cherish it, and the moments when you throw away your peace and comfort in pursuit of something else. You can begin to see when you keep your eye on your peace, and when you abandon your mindfulness of it.

Your here-and-now state is peace and comfort. Others share the same peace. Can you see that? Or are others around you throwing their peace away? From your awareness of your own peace, you can begin to watch what others do with theirs. You can begin to see how others throw their peace away.

This exercise has two names. I call it "Getting into the here and now" and also "Confessing my peace." I want you to get in the habit of doing this exercise many time throughout the day. For example, every time the clock comes around to twenty minutes after the hour, take out the paper where you've written these words and read them to yourself. Say them to yourself, and listen to your peace.

When you've heard it, you're ready to take your first step into your study of our interpersonal world. This study will show you how your negotiations and the wishes behind them tempt you to throw your personal peace away. You will see how your interpersonal habits tempt you with their promises. What promise could be so sweet? Confess your peace, here and now, and join me in the interpersonal world.

2

Interpersonal Operations

What do humans operate for? What is it that we negotiate for so continually between ourselves and others? The answer starts with another person giving birth to us. We come from a sea of amniotic fluid into a sea of interpersonal negotiations. Our world starts as an interpersonal world.

Do the fish see the sea? Do we humans who continually engage in interpersonal operations see our actions? Born into this interpersonal world, we remain so immersed in it that we but dimly sense its pervasive existence.

Once born, *the infant begins to operate on the mothering person*, and the mothering person responds with her own set of operations. Even as a newborn, the infant has a substantial set of operations. These operations affect the mother, and she responds. Anything the infant does may elicit a response from mother and so serve as operation.

Baby cries, wiggles, suckles, and sometimes remains quiet and gurgly. Very rapidly, baby grows able to do more operations. He soon smiles, coos, and begins to do things with his hands. With gaining strength he screams and does a set of things that we describe as anger. Less obviously, baby's littleness and helplessness affect the ways that mother responds. Baby soils and wets and these actions prompt operations by mother. Soon he learns to babble, to hold or drop objects. So it goes until baby says a first word, takes a first step, and stacks a first block.

I describe the forms of baby's operations with a few simple verbs. Baby is a *subject who acts*, not merely an object of others' actions. In fact, judging by parental responses, his operations appear omnipotent. By early childhood, baby-now-child operates by crying, whimpering, and sadding. He operates by performing, smiling, and stroking mother. He operates by pleasing, cooing, and helplessing. He operates by weaking, inepting, and soiling. Little one operates by messing and disarranging. He operates by hurting, suffering, and sicking. The child operates by angering, hitting, and beating. He operates with mother by fearing, anxietying, and stilling. He may operate by quieting.

Please notice that these operations by the infant, for the most part, involve throwing away his personal peace.

When baby begins to operate, mother responds according to her own characteristics. She may respond more to some operations and less to others, and not at all to some others. Mother's responses operate on the baby. *Her responses positively reinforce baby's operations* (remember Dr. B.F. Skinner). The operations that bring more response from mother become more frequent with our baby.

Mother's responses shape baby's set of operations. So baby may scream more often than he whimpers, or smile more than he shows fear. Over time, baby develops a whole set of ways for negotiating with mother. Baby then uses these same ways to negotiate with anyone else. Success with mother using an operation makes that operation part of baby's set of operations.

Significantly, the child develops this set of operations long before he can make his words stand for things. The child has a whole system for managing and negotiating with others, but he cannot talk about it. Not that child doesn't use a few words. But he uses his words for effect to gain a response rather than to convey data. His words are simply one more activity in his set of operations.

In this system for negotiating with the other people in his interpersonal world, the child uses the set of actions that got reinforcing responses from his mother. The interactions between infant-child and mother firmly establish this set of actions for managing mother. The child goes on to use this set of actions to manage others. The child completes this learning before he is five years old. He completes this learning before he can make his words stand for things.

I call the infant-child's set of actions *interpersonal habit.*

Please notice that the infant's interpersonal habit, for the most part, involves throwing away his personal peace.

Mother's operations on baby remarkably parallel baby's operations. Mother performs, coos, and strokes, as she cleans, dries, and nurses baby. She fears and anxieties and worries. She may scream or anger with him. She may strike or beat him. She may cry, sad, or helpless with him. She talks for effect to a baby who cannot yet talk. Mother's operations parallel baby's because *mother also learned to negotiate the interpersonal world as an infant-child.* Mother has an interpersonal habit set of her own.

Please note that mother's interpersonal habit, for the most part, involves her throwing away her personal peace.

The mother-infant relationship thus has a structure which we can describe. Mother and infant operate with parallel sets of operations. The relationship has symmetry. They frequently exchange roles. Sometimes the mother comforts the child and sometimes the child comforts the mother. All mother-infant operations show this symmetry.

The infant's experience of this relationship is that mother is always there. Even if she is momentarily unseen, mother will materialize when he operates. When he cries, mother materializes. If she didn't, the infant would not survive. In the mother-infant world, mother is always present. Thus the experience of separateness is not yet available to the infant in his mother-child interpersonal world.

Since the operations in this world do not involve referential speech, mother appears to know baby's state without being told. This appearance also obscures the fact of the baby's separateness and shows that he can manage mother without requests. Infant-child manages her with operations, not requests. Later in life this will become a problem. Each will assume that the other experiences the same thing, and this assumption will blind them to the need to tell each other what each experiences. When their separate experiences do not coincide, interpersonal habit will tempt them to try sadding to try to make their selves not separate.

For convenience, I define mother's *reinforcing response* to the baby-child operation as what baby *wishes* for. We can say that whatever baby operates for, he pursues a *wish* for. So we can rephrase their relationship by saying that mother knows baby's wishes without baby telling her. *Mother also learned her interpersonal habit as a baby-child.* So mother also sees her infant-child as knowing mother's wishes without her telling baby.

Baby wishes mother would pick him up, hold him, and dry him. He wishes she would warm him and nurse him at her breast. Baby wishes that mother would coo and lullaby. Similarly, mother wishes that baby would stroke her and relieve her engorged breast. Mother wishes that baby would coo, smile, and give her admiring looks.

In this world of give and take, they allow no one else. Mother gives the milk to only one. Mother appoints only one to relieve her breast. Both want an exclusive relationship. All others keep out! Later in life this becomes a problem. When other people enter, baby and even mother may begin to work at keeping the relationship exclusive. Interpersonal habit tempts them to cry or upset to get that wish. They throw away their peace.

This mother-infant relationship occurs completely as a direct, nonverbal experience. It involves no words that stand for things, and no future or past or other places enter into its logic. Thus it unfolds in the *here and now* and has no *time*. Promising a baby "milk tomorrow" will not work. Negotiating with a three-year-old by promising "we'll do it tomorrow" will not work. Beginning and ending and death do not exist in this world's timeless logic.

As the infant-child operates to manage mother for his wishes, a system of rights and wrongs develops. Right means that mother responds; wrong means that mother does not respond. So mother's response and mother's wishes delineate right and wrong. What mother wishes for becomes right and what mother wishes against becomes wrong.

Since crying, suffering, discontenting, and angering successfully get mother's best milk, all these actions subtly become *good*. Of course, mother and child don't overtly say that this is so, but they act as if it were. Since all such actions involve abandoning one's peace, throwing away one's peace becomes *good*. (Is this why many religious people say that suffering is good? Some say, "If you are not suffering you are not a Christian.")

In the Garden of Eden creation story, God declared the knowledge of good and evil forbidden. As in the myth, good and evil were not originally present in our earliest relationships. Yet the development of a unique and arbitrary view of good and evil is an inevitable consequence of our first interpersonal operations. The myth points out the perils of this inevitably arbitrary classification of things as good or evil. I have pointed out one of these perils: that we may subtly see abandoning our personal peace as *good*.

Since mother fulfills baby and baby fulfills mother,

they stick close together, perhaps even clinging to each other. We can say that they wish to stay physically close. Each operates to move toward the other.

In summary, mother and infant operate continually and symmetrically. They do not talk about their operations. They keep their relationship exclusive. The other's constant presence obscures their separateness. Without talk and words, they have no time and hence no future or past. Without words, they have no elsewhere. Without time, death and beginning and ending do not exist. They use a system of good and evil. They maintain physical closeness. Each appears to know the other's wishes without being told. Each appears to feel what the other feels. They relate as if there were only one organism.

When things don't go as they wish, both may throw away their personal peace to try to make things go as they wish. Remember, mother and infant do not talk referentially about their operations with each other. They do not report their operations or describe them. The whole system of the mother-infant world with its vigorous activity and its unique interpersonal habit remains unreported and *dimly seen*. Mother and infant-child do not know how they interact in their interpersonal world. They do not know that they are throwing away their personal peace to try to make things go as they wish.

Do the fish know about the sea? Probably not. Do mother and infant-child know about their interpersonal world? Definitely not. You and I started life in that same form of relationship. We started in the midst of a bustling set of here and now negotiations that proceeded unreported and unseen. Most of those operations involve throwing away personal peace.

All of us start in a mother-infant relationship where we learn a set of interpersonal habits. We practice that set of habits but we do not know about them. Most of these habits involve throwing away our personal peace. We cannot learn new ways to manage our interpersonal world well unless we learn about that world and learn to see it. *We can learn to give up abandoning our peace when we see that we abandon our peace.*

Have you confessed your peace recently?

3

Operating for Intermediate Responses

We aim for the fulfillment of the *sweetest wish*. We wish that mother hold us, cuddle us, and nurse us. In our infant negotiations we learn that mother first responds to our bids for attention by looking at us. She then responds by listening to us, and by moving toward us. Being nursed reinforces our bidding behavior. And all of mother's responses that lead to being nursed become reinforcers. Mother's looking, listening, moving toward us, and holding us become reinforcers. Once established as reinforcers, these responses by mother reinforce *independently* whether they lead to nursing or not. The baby learns to wish for and negotiate for these *intermediate responses* from mother.

If mother scowls or groans along with moving close to baby, picking up baby, and nursing baby, then mother's scowls or groans become reinforcers. Any response from mother that comes along with fulfillment of *the sweetest wish* can become a reinforcer. Even if mother responds by screaming at baby or smacking baby, then screams and smacks become reinforcers as well. Such intermediate responses become wished for with the same priority as the prime wish.

What does the infant do to operate with mother? How does he negotiate? How does he bid? He may cry or whine. He may smile or chuckle. He may scream or mess. He may babble or wiggle. Later he may anger.

Whatever the infant is doing is reinforced when mother responds by looking, listening, or coming close. Whatever bid the infant makes is reinforced when mother responds with holding and nursing. All of the infant's bids are reinforced by established intermediate reinforcers.

Performing, cuting, screaming, whimpering, or messing may all get the maternal response. Any or all of these behaviors may address her vulnerability and so become habatual negotiations. Successful behaviors become part of the infant's set of *interpersonal bids*, part of the infant's *interpersonal habit*.

When a path leads to the fulfillment of a wish, we end up wishing for the path itself. We end up seeking the path as we seek the wish. We seek it with the same vigor. So we can say that we wish to perform and to cute because these have succeeded in the past. We wish to scream, to whimper, or to mess because those behaviors have succeeded. The infant conducts countless interactions with mother, and from these interactions he develops a set of successful bids and paths. The infant develops a set of actions which he wishes to do. He wishes to do them because they have succeeded as paths to his prime wish.

Any infant operation can become such a wish, depending on the mother's characteristics. These *intermediate wish forms*, the operations that succeed, become part of the *interpersonal habit*. The child learns to do these operations before he can talk about things. His operations remain unreported as the prime wish remains unreported. Infants succeed most by doing things which abandon their personal peace. *Interpersonal habit consists mostly of actions that abandon personal peace.*

Since all of us begin with a mother-infant form of relationship, all of us come to attribute that form to all relationships. The *forms* of our infant operations persist throughout life. Only the *content* becomes more sophisticated with advancing age and increasing intellectual abilities. At later ages our operations may display the wish for power or the wish for attractiveness. These are sophisticated versions of the wish for attention. Our operations may display wishes for skills, money, and intelligence, or wishes for talent, physical strength, or goodness. These are sophisticated versions of the wish to perform and gain attention. Our operations may even display the wish to be bad. We exercise a sophisticated version of our wish for attention by wishing for a reprimand.

I could extend this list to an unwieldy length. Fortunately for people watchers, spotting the form of the wish unveils the operation underlying it. We can see what goes on without memorizing a long list.

The wish that mother see and hear us becomes the wish for *attention* and its many variations. We wish to appear attractive or to appear weak and helpless. We wish for fame or notoriety. We wish for intelligence and talent. Ostentatious goodness or provocative badness serve equally well to garner attention.

Many mothers respond vigorously to the infant's smiling, laughing, and appearing happy. This reinforces the infant's *happying* as a negotiation. The wish to happy may appear as smiling, laughing, singing. With later up-to-age content, the infant may show the wish to happy by saying, "You are a nice mommie." The infant may clap his hands or give mother a big hug. He may say, "This is a very nice day."

Mother may respond when infant-child offers her a bite of his cookie. This reinforces the infant's *sharing* as a negotiation. The wish to share may appear as infant trying to feed mother. Later the wish may show in the child saying, "Come look at the sunset with me." In another content, the child may say, "Come sit with me." With much later content, the wish to share may show in the request "Will you marry me?"

Most mothers respond quickly and reliably when the infant *angers*. Angering entails abandoning one's peace. Mother's response leads the infant to rely upon anger to get a sure response from mother. As our intellectual capacities grow, we may demonstrate the wish to anger as a wish to show irritation or to appear argumentative. We may engage in faultfinding, blaming, or prejudice. We may wish to appear temperamental, zealous, or fanatic. Negotiating with any of these actions entails abandoning one's personal peace.

Mother responds to and reinforces our weakness, helplessness, and incapability. So we learn to wish to be *helpless*. Later we sophisticate the form with up-to-age contents. The wish to be helpless appears as wishes to appear sick, poor, unintelligent, inept, or bungling. We wish to appear unkempt or underfed. We wish to appear beset with problems, helpless, struggling, or failing. All these negotiations entail throwing away one's peace.

Mother may respond to our submissive behavior. We learn to wish to be *submissive*. Later contents for this form show as wishes to cower or to grovel. We wish to play servant or slave, to please, or to placate. We wish to assume a subordinate role. Assuming this unpleasant role, we forsake any personal peace.

Most mothers respond to and reinforce the infant's suffering. We learn to wish to *suffer*. Later up-to-age and sophisticated content for this form show as wishes to appear sick or to have accidents. We wish to appear misused or abused. We wish to appear unfulfilled. We may learn to wish to appear attacked, beaten, maligned, or misunderstood. We may wish to suffer poor health. Again, this set of actions scrap our peace.

When mother responds to and thus reinforces our discontent, we learn to wish to *discontent*. With later sophisticated content the wish to discontent may show as wishes to spot blemishes. This wish may show as overlooking gratifications and opportunities. We may wish to underrate ourselves and others and to remain implacable. We may wish to find the speck in every apple pie. We may wish to avoid gratifications of the body by keeping our attention on discontenting self-talk or the TV. No personal peace can coexist with these actions.

When mother responds to and reinforces our fearing, we learn to wish to *fear*. With later up-to-age sophisticated content, the wish to fear may appear as the wish to put ourselves at risk. We may wish to spot danger everywhere and to overlook our comfortable and safe state. We may wish to appear deserted. We may wish to contemplate death and to report phobias. We may wish to go insane or to lose control. We may wish to regard gratification as dangerous. We may wish to keep in touch with all the horrors of the whole world. We may wish to have a bodily breakdown, to merit condemnation, or to fear being afraid. No one can see any personal peace midst all these activities.

When I talk to myself, I tell myself whatever I wish to hear. When you talk to yourself you tell yourself whatever you wish yourself to hear. People may call this thinking, but the term self-talk portrays this act more accurately and practically. What can I expect to hear me say to myself? I can expect me to say things that fulfill my wishes. You can expect you to say things to yourself that fulfill your wishes.

Let's assume that you and I have learned to wish all the wishes that I have described developing in infant-children. Let's assume that we later supply sophisticated content. We can then expect to hear ourselves tell ourselves (in some sophisticated content) that we wish to have attention, to happy, or to share. We say we wish to perform, to anger, or to helpless. We tell ourselves we wish to submit, to suffer, to discontent, and to fear. In our preoccupation with affecting others with these unpleasantries, we never tell ourselves that we exist in peace.

Let's take these examples of such self-talk one by one.

When we wish for attention, we tell ourselves that we will become a famous country singer. (We call some self-talk daydreaming.) Or we tell ourselves that our clothes are a mess. (We call some self-talk worrying.)

When we wish to happy, we tell ourselves how good our dinner is. We tell ourselves that our wife is the best woman in the world. We tell ourselves that we have a very enjoyable and challenging job. We tell ourselves how good it feels to hug our friends. We tell ourselves that we love the birds and flowers in the yard. We may even confess our peace.

When we wish to share, we tell ourselves we must call our friend. We tell ourselves, "I must remember to tell Mary that a goldfinch was at her feeder." We tell ourselves "I will take this book to my friend." Later we may tell ourselves, "I would like to make love with Mary." We may tell ourselves, "I would like to marry Mary." Even later we may tell ourselves, "I want to have a baby." We may tell ourselves, "I want to confess my peace to Mary."

When we wish to perform, we tell ourselves that we are the best tennis players on the block. Or we tell ourselves that we will make a million bucks. We may tell ourselves things we can do to help others. We may tell ourselves that we will write the book of the century. We may tell ourselves how important we are to support and comfort others. We may even admit that we exist in peace.

When we wish to anger, we tell ourselves that Congress is crooked. Or we tell ourselves that our spouse is insensitive. We tell ourselves that the sermon today was terrible. We tell ourselves that our social group should have a better organization. We tell ourselves that the U.S. should drop an A-bomb on the Arabs. We tell ourselves that the world needs total reform. We tell ourselves that the auto mechanic padded his bill to gouge us. Such angering self-talk excludes any talk of personal peace.

When we wish to helpless, we tell ourselves that we cannot fix things around the house. We tell ourselves that we cannot cook. We tell ourselves that things are too complex for us to understand. We tell ourselves that we are not intelligent. We tell ourselves that we have weak eyes or weak muscles. This unpleasant self-talk abandons any acknowledgement of personal peace.

When we wish to submit, we may tell ourselves that we enjoy pleasing the supervisor. We tell ourselves to defer all decisions to our spouse. We tell ourselves that we cannot lead a group but that we can be a valuable group member. We tell ourselves that we cannot lead but that we are good followers. We tell ourselves to watch carefully for hints of other's wishes. This tedium of watching for the other to say "jump" robs us from entertaining any talk of personal peace.

When we wish to suffer, we tell ourselves that our spouse may leave us. (We call some self-talk worrying.) We talk to ourselves about our son who was killed and how great is our loss. (We call some self-talk grief.) We tell ourselves that our children risk having an accident or falling prey to dope peddlers. We tell ourselves that our money will not go far enough to provide well for us. We tell ourselves that our body will probably fall victim to cancer or a heart attack. We tell ourselves that we are ashamed of our many shortcomings. We tell ourselves of our embarrassment at not remembering someone's name when we met them. We tell ourselves that we are poor miserable sinners. (We do this righteously, of course.) With this self-talk of the tragic we prevent any consideration of personal peace. We forget to confess our peace!

When we wish to discontent, we tell ourselves that the food at dinner was unsavory. We tell ourselves that our spouse is too messy. We tell ourselves that our supervisor does not appreciate us and that he is incompetent anyway. We tell ourselves that sunny weather is hot and rainy weather is bad weather. We tell ourselves that work is a rat race. (Thank God it's Friday.) We tell ourselves that the world is all fouled up. We tell ourselves that our Congressmen are prostitutes to the lobbyists. We forget to confess our peace! We cannot discontent and admit to any personal peace.

When we wish to fear, we tell ourselves that burglars may break into our house tonight (in spite of our $5000 burglar alarm system). We tell ourselves that we are bound to catch AIDS from the grocery sacks. We tell ourselves that our Christianity is flawed. We tell ourselves that the Russians will probably attack. We tell ourselves that our teenagers will have an auto crash. We tell ourselves that we can't stand the sight of frogs. (We then say that there is probably a frog in the patio flower pot.) We tell ourselves that our heart may fail to beat. (We had better feel our pulse to see if it is still beating.) We tell ourselves that no publisher will ever accept our book. (No prophet receives acceptance in his time.) We tell ourselves that we will discover our own irreparable flaw in this book and that finding it will ruin our life. (Quick, throw the book away.) We forget to confess our peace! Fearing prevents any admission of personal peace.

These sayings that we tell ourselves are exactly what we report to others. We tell them these same things when we pursue our wishes through them. For example, we ply our wishes with others by reporting that we are the best tennis player on the block (performing). We ply our wishes with others by telling them how good dinner is (happying). We ply our wishes by asking them to look at the sunset with us (sharing). We ply our wishes by telling them the auto mechanic is crooked (angering). We tell them that we can't cook (helplessing). We tell them to take over the family finances (submitting). We tell them how they hurt us by neglect (suffering). We tell them that the weather is too hot (discontenting). We tell them that we fear that a frog jumped into the flower pot (fearing.) Most of these ways of negotiating with others involve abandonment of personal peace. Of course, we never, never confess our peace to them!

Have you confessed your peace recently?

4

Recipe for People Watchers

Mapping out our interpersonal world resembles mapping out an elephant. We can walk around the elephant and make one map from this aspect and another from that aspect. We map until we have a fistful of maps. Finally, the map reader must put all these maps together before he can get a comprehensible view of the elephant.

Showing an elephant works better than a thousand maps. We can point to the elephant. We can encourage our disciple to walk around and view the elephant. The disciple then gains a coherent view of the elephant.

Similarly, I can map different aspects of interpersonal negotiations and the interpersonal world and depend on you, the map reader, to put all these maps together into a coherent whole. Fortunately, with interpersonal operations, we need not rely on maps. The real thing lives and breathes all around us. Interpersonal relations continually exercise their mechanisms for you and I to look at and see. There lies the challenge. *Before you can look at and see these interpersonal operations, you must learn how to look at and how to see them.*

We need no maps of an elephant when we have an elephant. We need no maps of interpersonal operations when we have interpersonal operations going on around us continually. The maps I draw here merely serve as pointers to invite you to look where you have never looked before. The maps in this book invite you to look in ways that you have never looked before.

Seeing always depends on how you look. The Eskimo sees 32 snows, where I only see one snow. He knows how to look.

The "how to look" of people-watching hinges on your learning to *get into the here and now*. (Have you confessed your peace recently? Please do that exercise now.) Interpersonal operations go on in the here and now. When you fix your attention on thoughts of five minutes ago, you cannot see the living operation. We can talk to ourselves about five minutes ago, a day ago, or a year ago, but what we talk about no longer exists. When you fix your attention on thoughts of places other than your present location, you cannot see the living operation. The operation does not exist outside this room. *Here and now*, I operate with you and you with me. We can see each other only in this split second of now.

We grasp the here and now with our senses, a direct, nonverbal experience. That experience evaporates the instant we begin to entertain *any self-talk*. The secret hides in knowing to look here and now. This entails sacrificing our beloved habit of perpetually talking to ourselves.

Our self-talk and our talk with others *serves our interpersonal habit*. Our thoughts portray the interpersonal world as the one that we prevailed over as an infant-child. Our thoughts depict a world where we could depend on attention getting or happying to get others to do our wishes. Or where we could depend on sharing or angering, or helplessing or submitting, or suffering or discontenting, or fearing and abandoning our peace to get others to do what we wished. In that infant-child world we worked so continually at these operations which we could not talk about that they seemed to occupy the whole universe. We saw no peace in that universe. We were so preoccupied with the pursuit of our wishes through these operations that we never experienced our state as peace and comfort.

That world has gone. Its ways of thinking enslave us

in illusion.

Now please confess your peace again with me.

When we forsake our self-talk and fix our attention steadfastly on the here and now, we begin to see the living present. We see operations occurring before our eyes, within reach of all our senses. *Here-and-now looking* unveils our illusions. We begin to see what we never before saw, right under our noses. We grasp the experience with our senses and without words.

Looking without words, you can see me whimper or whine to negotiate with you. You can see me present an image of myself as deprived to negotiate with you. You can see me anger to negotiate with you. When I happy to negotiate with you, you can spot my happying. And I can see whatever you do to negotiate with me. *Nothing is hidden*. You can see the temptations to ignore any peace each time we present some form of discontent as a bid for what we wish from each other.

Please confess your peace again with me.

When we focus our attention in the small space and in the split second between me and you, we begin to see. We see what we do with each other. You see me *performing* now to evoke a nurturing response from you. My writing serves as content for the performing operation that I am doing with you here and now. How do you respond? However you respond, you operate to evoke a nurturing response from me. Are you surprised? You may respond with affection, irritation, disdain, or incredulity. Your response operates with me at this moment. Did you know you did that? When you grasped your response, you began to see!

Small changes in language can help simplify the seeing of interpersonal operations. The world of interpersonal operations dawns before we have the capacity for making our words stand for something. And after we gain the capacity for referential speech, we almost never talk about these operations. As a result, many words we need to describe interpersonal operations are absent from our language.

Since interpersonal operations are actions, *we can*

best describe them with action verbs.

Here is a partial lexicon of active verbs useful in describing interpersonal operations.

acts abused with
acts misused with
angers with
anxieties with
argues with
beats with
blames with
brags with
bungles with
can't eat with
chases with
clowns with
competes with
complains with
coos with
copulates with
cries with
defers with
depresses with
disarranges with
dissatisfies with
discontents with
embarrasses with
entertains with
faints with
fears with
fights with
flirts with
fondles with
frustrates with
fusses with
guilts with
happies with

headaches with
helplesses with
heroes with
hits with
hostiles with
hugs with
hurts with
inepts with
inferiors with
invites with
joys with
kisses with
laughs with
low self-esteems
    with
martyrs with
messes with
murders with
obsesses with
passive aggresses
    with
performs with
phobics with
pleases with
pouts with
puzzles with
quiets with
rages with
runs away with
sads with
screams with
self-mutilates
    with

self-depreciates
    with
self-reveals with
self-displays with
shames with
shares with
shows off with
shies with
sicks with
sillies with
smiles with
soils with
stills with
stomachaches
    with
strokes with
struggles with
submits with
suffers with
suicides with
tantrums with
teases with
tickles with
unables with
victims with
vomits with
weaks with
whimpers with
whines with
withdraws with
won't eat with
yells with

Interpersonal operations always take place between two persons. Jane operates *with* Dick and Dick operates *with* Jane. They negotiate *with* each other. So we can describe interpersonal operations by using *an active verb* usually followed by the preposition *with*.

Some of these new verbs may baffle you a little at first (for example, *inferiors with* or *dissatisfies with*). Just remember that a person always does some action *with* another person. The person acts out his inferiority or dissatisfaction here and now for a desired response from the other.

You will notice that many of these operations entail abandonment of your personal peace.

I could group these specific verbs under more general categories such as *inferiors*, *discontents*, *angers*, and *performs*. But specific verbs will make it simpler to spot operations. When someone says, "I am a dope," we easily recognize that he *self-depreciates*. We might have trouble spotting that he *inferiors*, until we become used to the term. We then can see that *bungling*, *deferring*, *inepting*, and *weaking* are all actions designed to *inferior* us into responding according to the wishes of this grownup infant-child.

A sentence describing an operation has a subject doing an action (a verb) with another subject. In the grammar of operations, *both* parties are subjects. Both participate actively, even though only one is the grammatical subject of the sentence. When Tim *screams with* Sarah, he does so by raising his voice. Whatever Sarah's response is, it becomes part of the same operation. Tim *screams with* Sarah and Sarah *screams with* Tim.

Interpersonal operations always occur between two subjects. When you cast the second person as object, you fall into the illusion that that person is merely the passive recipient of another's actions. It's tempting to see ourselves as objects. We all begin with a mother-infant relationship in which mother acts upon the infant. We're picked up, fed, comforted, and these things simply happen to us, as if by a kind of magic or irresistible force. Many of the sentences we use still reflect this view. We say, "Life has been hard on me." The structure of the sentence turns us into a helpless object with no control over our lives.

The preposition *with* helps us remember that the second person always acts in a subject role. "Mary talked with Robert" reminds us that Robert is not just a passive object that Mary acts upon. The expanded sentence "Robert talks with Mary talks with Robert" lets us see that both are subjects with an active role in what they do with each other.

"Person A operates with person B" is the general form of interpersonal operations. The corresponding operation "Person B operates with person A" follows. The two act thus as long as they relate with each other.

Since we can see interpersonal operations only in the here and now, we have use only for present-tense active verbs. Present-tense verbs point us toward the here and now. Concentrated looking at our actions here and now leads to seeing.

Once seen, interpersonal operations, like our once-seen elephant, can never elude us any more.

Please confess your peace again. Once seen, your peace can never elude you unless you fall to the temptations of old interpersonal habit. You may momentarily obscure your personal peace by discontenting as a bid for me to do your wishes. Once you have soundly confronted your personal peace, you may find yourself skeptical of your discontenting. You may suspect that your peace lurks in the background patiently waiting for you to have your discontenting binge. Under the warmth of your skepticism, your discontenting may fade. You may return to an admission of personal peace. The discontenting will cease.

5

Low Self-Esteeming

When you as an infant made your first fumbling attempts to hold your spoon, mother and father quickly helped you. When you made your first fumbling attempts to stand, mother and father jumped to assist you. A thousand fumbling attempts met helping responses from mother or father.

Unnoticed in all this interaction is the fact that your parents' responses strongly reinforced your not-doing, your helplessing. Mothers and fathers inevitably train baby to *get a response by failing to do*. As a child you obtained extensive reinforcement for being weak, poorly coordinated, and helpless. In a very real way, you *learned* to drop your spoon and fall down. Baby may even suddenly lose his ability to walk after he has walked well for weeks. You learned to use all manner of can't-do behaviors in a hundred different ways.

In their child's babyhood or early infancy, the parents can pick baby up when he falls down and readily amend all the other many small mistakes. But as the child grows older and more sophisticated, he introduces new contents for this form of operating on his parents. He devises bigger and better ways of *helplessing* as a bid for parental response. He fails his high school courses.

In this way, the child develops a dependence on his

inferiorities in strength and capability. He depends on helplessing as an operation for parental response. He clings to this image of an inferior, flawed self and ignores any outside evidence against it. While busily helplessing, the child finds no utility in paying attention to his personal peace.

We call this use of helplessing and inferiority "low self-esteeming." We do not *have* low self-esteem. We *do* it. So I make the operation into a verb, to show that I negotiate with you by *low self-esteeming* to bid you to do my wishes. Meanwhile my personal peace lies completely unattended and for practical purposes nonexistent.

Low self-esteeming grows from these subtle childhood origins to end up pervading our interpersonal negotiations. Our interpersonal habit remembers that low self-esteeming received a parental response. Dim memories of being picked up, comforted, and held form an unseen backdrop that promotes our confidence in that habit. And now, in many other interactions, we depend on low self-esteeming to get a parental response from the other person. Low self-esteeming becomes a broad aspect of our interpersonal world.

Have you ever noticed that public speakers usually begin their presentations with some self-disparaging remark? In that remark, you witnessed low self-esteeming. Have you tried to give a compliment to someone lately? Do you notice how often the other person brushes the compliment aside as though it had something contaminating about it? Again, you witnessed low self-esteeming.

We actively low self-esteem. It is not a state. You have to keep working at low self-esteeming or it vanishes. And the child's dependence on the image of an inferior self recreates itself in the self-disparagement of the public speaker and in the adult's refusal to accept even the mildest of compliments.

Have you noticed yourself making self-disparaging remarks? Have you noticed yourself brushing off compliments? Watch carefully and you will spot your own low self-esteeming.

Remember that as an infant-child you developed a set of actions for managing your significant others. You developed this set of habitual negotiations before you could speak. So you could not talk about your interpersonal habit. By the time you could speak, the process that led to your interpersonal habit had long since passed. So even then you still could not and did not talk about your interpersonal negotiations. Yet this habitual set of actions holds in your interpersonal negotiations throughout your life. You remain blind to your interpersonal world — or at least until you learn to see your habits for what they are.

The sophistication of later life brings sophisticated contents to the forms of negotiation, but the forms remain the same. We grow more creative at slighting ourselves, at lowering our self-worth in subtle ways, but the old dependence on the childish self-image with its comforting parental response remains exactly the same. Those who know how to look for the form can see the face of the child and hear what he negotiates for.

The cultural rule that one must not speak favorably of oneself shows how pervasive that habit is. In our society, we work at self-depreciation as though it were the purest labor of righteousness. We devise the most fetching contents for our attacks on ourselves. We claim our inferiority in many creative ways. We say, "I just can't cook." Or we say, "Machines baffle me."

Low self-esteeming correlates with a group of kindred forms of negotiation. We learn to negotiate by *helplessing* and *sicking* through the same types of interaction that taught us to low self-esteem. *Complexing* means seeing things as being so complex that we cannot fathom or deal with them. Intellectuals frequently practice this subtle form of helplessing. *Obsessing, phobicking*, and *worrying* can all keep us from doing anything at all. All of these low self-esteeming, helplessing, can't-do operations bid for the same parental response. All of them contribute to a robust self-depreciation.

Operating by *performing* for a parental response tends to offset the can't-do operations. A performing operation gains parental purrs when mother and father respond to baby's first smile. Mother and father respond when baby says his first words. They respond when he takes his first step. As the infant-child develops more capacities, his parents continue to reinforce his performances. Some children receive more of this reinforcing notice from their parents; others receive less. The parents' interpersonal styles determine to what extent the child will learn to *negotiate by performance*.

Note that this negotiation does not necessarily bar personal peace. It can if the child becomes so dependent on performing that he cannot allow himself a moment's respite.

The *catch them doing something good* parent will reinforce the performing aspect of the child's interpersonal negotiations. The child learns that doing *good* will get a parental response. "Good" means some performance that gets parental response. "Good" means something the parent wishes the child to do.

In a sense, the child operates on the parents just like he operates on his blocks. He tries this and he tries that. Just as he learns the characteristics of his blocks, so he learns the characteristics of his parents.

When parents restrict the child's operative explorations on things, they restrict the child's mastery of things. When parents restrict the child's explorations of themselves, they restrict the child's interpersonal habit.

Unnecessarily restrictive parents give the child a view that the main problem consists of handling, and watching out for his parents. Parental restrictions teach the child that the significance of other persons overshadows the significance of the object world. The child's world ends up consisting of ninety percent other person. Only ten percent of his world is left over for blocks and bugs and flowers and cool gooey mud. This shrunken world is created when the parent *catches the child doing bad* and steps in to supervise little one's every move. And the unexplored outside world seems inhospitable, threatening, and remote. Always on the look out, the child has no time for personal peace.

Just how careful do you have to be about others moment by moment? Do you incessantly concern yourself with what others will think? Do you abandon your peace to remain cautious about how others will respond to you?

The parent can arrange the environment to allow the child free exploration. The parent *can tolerate the child's operations on the parent with good humor and without becoming upset.* This arrangement provides a quite different interpersonal habit to the child. This child's world consists of fifty percent other person. And a second, expanding fifty percent contains all the blocks and bugs and flowers and cool gooey mud. The child can explore the world, since he doesn't have to guard against his parents' restrictions. He can operate on his parents without expecting an outburst or a rebuke. And the explored outside world seems inviting, challenging, and within reach.

The child with an inviting world will try more and more operations. And the parent will have more and more opportunities to catch the child doing good. These new responses in turn reinforce the child's habit of exploring and investigating and performing.

Parents have another opportunity to shape their children's interpersonal habit during the formative years. Catch your children being. Respond when they do nothing in particular. Pick them up, hold them, and hug them. Make over them for no other reason than that they *are*. This *nonspecific reinforcement* imparts an interpersonal view that asserts: "Others value me." It imparts an interpersonal view that "My presence has value." It allows attention to personal peace.

Few persons know the value of their presence. Few of us have had the experience that I have described—an experience that allows us to realize that we give when we give our presence. Instead, for so many, all the kindred forms of helplessing and low self-esteeming overshadow this potential value that we have.

I have often questioned people and seldom found this realization of the value of personal presence. By contrast, every person that I have known has had a well-developed set of low self-esteeming negotiations.

I want you to begin to watch for your low self-esteeming operations. You will gradually begin to spot them. As you spot these operations, you will be able to become skeptical of them. You will will turn from "I can't" to "I probably can." You will turn from "I don't admire me" to "I am an interesting, capable, and lovable person." You will turn from seeing yourself as inferior to seeing yourself as uniquely different. You will cease seeing difference as inferiority.

6

Word Operations

After we reach twelve years of age, we gain our full capabilities to use words. From this time, we begin to use words to express all our old forms of interpersonal habit. We use our words to operate with and negotiate with others. Our interpersonal habit appears cloaked in words and words become the chief veil which hides our personal peace.

As children, we whined. When we become verbal, we complain about the weather. As children, we helplessed. When we become verbal, we say, "Cooking is beyond me." As children, we screamed. When we become verbal, we say, "The sight of a frog makes me panic." As children, we struck out in anger. When we become verbal, we say, "You make me mad." As children, we dropped our fork. When we become verbal, we say, "What can you expect from someone inept like me."

We can use words to practice every form of our interpersonal habit. Most of these old habits keep us from any discovery of our peaceful state. In this way, words become the chief matrix of temptation away from seeing your state of personal peace.

Many insights lay hidden in our words waiting for you and I to ferret them out. All these insights relate to our interpersonal negotiations. Frequently they relate to how we manage to avoid our personal peace.

Baby humans begin to babble at a very early age. Parental reinforcement encourages them to experiment until they come to utter something recognizably similar to the parent's talk. By age two to three, their vocal skill increases to the point that we say, "They talk." Parents take their five-year-old's ability to talk as a matter of course.

An unseen fact lurks behind all this seemingly adult talking by our little one. The child uses his vocal behaviors as operations because his words frequently *produce an effect*. His words exercise a kind of magic: they bring a parental response that fulfills his wishes. (This parallels the child's experience that falling down magically produces someone to pick him up.) The child's interpersonal view becomes: "Words produce an effect with others."

In the child's interpersonal habit, no element of truth or falsehood exists with words. We experience no surprise when our little one says, "A lion jumped in my window." We recognize his operation as a bid to sleep in mother's room. And his words either produce an effect or they don't. The truth or falsehood of the bid has nothing to do with its success or failure.

We all have a certain familiarity with the use of words for effect. But few of us realize that *all of our words* serve that same function.

We use words first and always to produce an effect in the other person. We do operations on each other with words. We use words just like we use any other behavior. We use words to produce an effect whether we speak them, write them, or sign them.

Since words are always intended to produce an effect, *we cannot expect that any given set of words refers to anything tangible*. In fact, much talk doesn't. You need to know this. You can't expect that every set of words you hear or read actually refers to something. Otherwise, you will think that you are receiving information when, in fact, you are not.

You may begin to suspect that your companion's words convey no information. Be careful! Your wish for information (where there is none) may tempt you to abandon your peace and resort to interpersonal habits to try for your wish. You may begin to anger to try to get your companion to supply you with your wish. Out goes your peace. Or you may call upon some other old reliable interpersonal habit to bid for the information you expect. Whether you get it or not, you are likely to abandon sight of your personal peace.

We develop the capacity to use words referentially at about age five. The six-year-old can make his words stand for something. So besides negotiating for effect, he can then use his words to point to things. He can make a report about himself and his world such as "I left the bananas in the kitchen." We call this the ability to *symbolize*. The words he uses stand for something, and when he uses them others know what things or happenings or situations the words are pointing to.

Much opportunity for failure of reference exists when we speak together. When we have not agreed on the referents of terms, we frequently lose sight of a clear reference for our words. We think we are saying something to each other when, in fact, we are not. When I say "faith," you will hear what the term faith references for you. The word may very well mean something very different for me. We may tell ourselves that we understood each other when we only exchanged verbal nonsense. When we begin to suspect that we didn't understand each other, we may be tempted to resort to old negotiation habits which scrub personal peace.

We can make sure our maps reference only by taking time to share a common experience. We can then agree to reference that common experience by a word or set of words. We can do this negotiation of reference about things or situations. We thus can avoid the derailment of attempts to share information and the temptation to resort to negotiation habits which shuck peace.

Sharing information is basically a peaceful negotiation. But when we begin to fail the sharing negotiation, non-peaceful forms of negotiation tempt us.

The pointing or referring function of words never exists alone. This function always coexists with the for-effect function. This referential function has no independent existence like the for-effect function does.

When the five-year-old gains the capacity to let words stand for things, he can then name things. Nevertheless, he cannot yet speak as an adult can. Children are *not little adults*. As a parent, you need to know that you are not talking to a small adult. This will enable you to exercise patience with children. This will help you avoid the temptation to throw away your peace to try to make adult talk possible with them.

At about age eleven, the child's adult cognitive capacities have arrived and show him a delightfully amplified view of the world. An eleven-year-old can match wits with the adults, though sometimes at a slight disadvantage for lack of experience.

You need to know this so you can begin to enjoy adult conversation with those over twelve years old. You can leave off dealing with them as children and unwittingly putting them down. Seeing young adults as equals will put your relating with them on a respectful footing. You can begin true adult friendships. You can avoid the temptation to return to old negotiation habits that abandon peace in the relationship.

If a child's parents have encouraged exploration of the world since his infancy, his interpersonal habit calls for exploration. With his new capacities, he now has a whole spectrum of new territories to explore. Especially, he can now explore the interpersonal arena. He begins to explore by all manner of new operations. For example, he experiments with leading others or following others. He experiments with asking for a date or introducing one person to another.

Our youngster must explore and grasp and master hundreds of interpersonal situations before he can negotiate the interpersonal world well. We take these things for granted, but they occupy much of the youth's attention and energy. Young adults study and learn much outside the prescribed school curriculum, much that stands of equal or greater importance.

Knowing about such exploring helps parents to remain partners in their offspring's becoming. Knowing this helps parents not to insist that the youth attend only to curriculum. Knowing this helps the parents to avoid temptation to use old negotiation habits. Knowing this helps them avoid trying to make the youth do and be exactly as they wish.

The wish that another do and be exactly as I wish is an impossible wish. When we pursue impossible wishes, we resort to old reliable negotiation habits such as suffering or angering or helplessing. In this we abandon personal peace.

When the youth has gained adult capacities, he gains new perception. Many of these perceptions are made possible by his capacity for referential speech and all the uses of thought and logic that go with it to make up the symbolic world. At this age, much attention is given to classifying and categorizing experience according to some set of all the many various available codes. "This makes sense," he says. Or "That just isn't cool." His standards may change frequently, but his interest in his new abilities remains. And so he talks about the new territories that he explores and reports his activities in them.

This attention to experience contrasts with his *interpersonal habit*, which came to him long before he could speak referentially. Hence he does not talk about or report this aspect of his behavior. Yet his interpersonal habit operates, even though unreported. No matter how sophisticated the subject matter of our person's verbiage, his talk serves his interpersonal operations.

Do the fishes see the sea? Do we see the interpersonal world with its constant set of interpersonal negotiations? Do we see these negotiations conducted against the backdrop of interpersonal habit which they serve? Do we see how most actions of interpersonal habit prevent grasping our personal peace?

A businessman sits eating his steak in an elegant restaurant. By his girth we can see that he lives in bounty. We listen to his conversation with his fellow businessman. He tells a very convincing tale. Our nation and the world are crumbling. He speaks eloquently of problem after problem. Bad news dominates his talking. He remains oblivious to his peaceful state. I want you to learn by watching how he uses words.

His words may seem incongruent on the surface. His affluence may seem incongruent with his discontent. But remember that he negotiates with his companion. Remember that he negotiates according to his interpersonal habit. Remember that as a child his whining succeeded in achieving parental response. Now we begin to see this man's interpersonal habit. What worked for him at age one or two? Whining got him comforted and held and fed. So he uses a sophisticated content for his whining form. He operates with his companion by whining. He whines out all his bad news. His interpersonal habit says that this will succeed. His true state of comfort and pleasurable eating remains unattended. His personal peace remains unattended.

Does he know what he does? Do fishes see the sea? He cannot talk about his negotiations or report them since they developed before he could talk. Does he see what he does? Do the fishes see the sea?

It will help to see word operations clearly if we start by contrasting them with the here-and-now tangible world. We cannot put the here-and-now world into words. We must apprehend it by our five senses. We experience it uniquely and cannot tell another that experience. Another cannot climb into your skin and know what you experience there. You can send word reports about your here-and-now world. Another can understand what you say about your world, but no one can see it with your eyes, or hear it with your ears, or feel it on your fingertips. No one can get inside you. *There remains a wide and unbridgeable gulf between your experienced here-and-now world and mine.*

Remember that in the mother-infant relation there seemed to be no separateness. In fact, we all have a strong wish not to be separate from the other. This wish finds expression in statements like "no man is an island." Nevertheless that unbridgeable gulf remains between your experience and my experience. We may find ourselves pursuing this impossible wish against separateness with old interpersonal habit. Out goes our personal peace. Recognizing our separateness and difference must precede gaining the ability to steadfastly entertain our personal peace.

Consider your here-and-now world. Probably you do not hunger or thirst. Probably you do not feel uncomfortable warmth or cold. Probably you do not feel pain. No one attacks you at the moment. So we might say that you experience a world of *peace and comfort* here and now.

Any glimpse of this peaceful, comfortable state sends people scurrying for some way of saying "This is illusion." The remote possibility that *peace* and *comfort* may dominate the here and now generates prompt action. They act promptly to bring the situation into line with interpersonal habit. That habit says: "Discomfort gets you fed. Flee from this perverting vision of peace and comfort." *Notice that they depend on words to distract and avoid facing their peace.*

This is exactly why you need to know and fathom much about words and language. Words chiefly serve interpersonal habit to distract and avoid facing personal peace.

How can you escape, now that I have confronted you with your here-and-now state of personal peace? The solution lies in concentrating on words. We can use our facility with words to blot out that glimpse of peace and comfort.

We can quickly remind ourselves in words of the many items of bad news that we have savored in the preceding hours. We then witness the power of our facility with words. We witness that this power serves inter-personal habit and coincidently hides any peace.

Until you learn better, interpersonal habit prevails. Our sophisticated *word operations* serve interpersonal habit. We devote our word skills and creativity to recreate the world just the way our interpersonal habit knew it. This collusion between word skills and inter-personal habit presents us with a view of life that blinds us to all else.

Do the fishes see the sea? Do we see that our words governed by interpersonal habit present us with an anachronism? Do we see that our words governed by interpersonal habit present us an illusion? Do we see that our words governed by interpersonal habit paint a world where discomfort means success? Do we see that they paint a world where peace and comfort mean nothing? Do the fishes see the sea?

The forms of infant operations take on sophisticated word contents when our capacity for word artistry develops. The infant operates with crying, whimpering, and sadding. The infant operates with performing, coo-ing, stroking, and pleasing mother. The infant operates with helplessing, weaking, inferioring, and low self-esteeming. He operates with soiling, messing, and disar-ranging. He operates with hurting, suffering, and sicking. He operates with angering, hitting, and beating. He oper-ates with fearing and anxietying. He operates with still-ing and quieting.

The youth-adult uses words to perform all of these operations. The youth-adult commands his words with artistic skill. He can say, "My teacher isn't fair," and the old operation of whining is presented for negotiation. He can helpless and anger and fear with his words. Personal peace remains unattended.

Still he cannot report or talk about the set of opera-tions in his interpersonal habit. He cannot report the operations because they developed well before he could report. The person he talks to cannot report them either for the same reason. They negotiate but they do not talk about their negotiations.

We use the infant operations clothed in sophisticated words to make our bids in our interpersonal negotiations. The other person responds according to his interpersonal habit. He may respond with a complementary behavior and to an extent fulfill our wish. He may respond with a contentious counterbid of his own. With his particular interpersonal habit, he may simply not recognize our bid as a bid. He may not have the experience to recognize it.

Interpersonal negotiations proceed by bid and counterbid and an occasional wish-fulfilling response. One may *whimper* as a bid: "My wife doesn't understand me." The other may *whimper* back as a counterbid: "Mine doesn't understand me either." Notice that both bid for the infant role. Both bid that the other take care of them. They compete, and their negotiation doesn't work.

Then one counterbids: "Let's go down to the pub and have a beer to the sorry plight of husbands." The other accepts and they go down and operate by *suffering* together. Neither sees any personal peace here. They follow the interpersonal habit that suffering brings those maternal ministrations which they have not negotiated from each other.

The use of words makes our interpersonal negotiations appear complex. All the thousands of things we hear people say make it seem like there are thousands of possible bids. In fact, our interpersonal habit consists of a small number of operations. When we learn to see through the words, we find that interpersonal habit employs only about ten kinds of operation. When we look at these operations, we see the simplicity of our negotiations. *Most of these operations obviate seeing personal peace.*

Mother takes care of us. She provides the *sweetest experience* that we humans find in life. She picks us up and holds us. She cuddles us and makes us comfortable.

She nurses us at the breast. She imprints us with a knowledge of the sweetest experience. All operations in interpersonal habit bid for that set of mothering responses.

The interpersonal habit that we see in any adult's operations show *what succeeded for him as an infant negotiator*. He uses what used to work. The intensity of his operating shows how intensely he had to operate to succeed. He uses today what worked to get that sweetest experience during infancy and early childhood. In that sense, interpersonal negotiations aim for that sweetest experience. The most sophisticated professed aims all trace back to that experience.

Remember my project to teach you to read interpersonal negotiations? How convenient that we use so few negotiation forms. How convenient that those few negotiation forms all aim for a simple sweetest experience. You can see that we probably will succeed.

We start with a mother-infant relationship and we attribute that same form to subsequent relationships. We work at keeping our relationships in that form. We notice that work as an aspect of interpersonal habit.

When we use words, you may notice that we often structure our sentences with an impersonal or obscure subject. For example, we say, "The world is a wearisome world." This shows the *subservience of language structure to interpersonal habit*. When I use a sentence with an impersonal subject, I describe the event as if it were happening *to* me. I describe myself as the recipient of the event. I place myself in an *infant role*. This sentence structure conceals the active operating role of the person speaking. Speaking this way, we structure our words to cast the relationship into the mother-infant form. Seldom does this form admit any peace.

We do not say, "I wish you would not do that." That structure paints clearly who does the doing. Instead, we say, "You hurt my feelings." The hurt-feeling operation keeps the speaker in an infant role. This aspect shows clearly when a person says, "You made me feel happy."

Here the speaker clearly describes himself as a receiving infant.

We structure our language to fit our interpersonal habit and keep a mother-infant form for our relationships. Sentence structure, syntax, and the terms we employ all show this subservience to interpersonal habit.

Many words in our language exist solely for operating and for producing an effect. These *operator* words do not refer to anything tangible. For example, no tangible or observable referent exists for the term "hurt feelings." No one can point their finger to where they hurt. We say "hurt feelings" to produce an effect. We say "hurt feelings" to bid for the other to stop what they do and do what we wish instead.

Many highly general or abstract words are entirely operational. These words bid for an effect and do not refer to anything tangible. Terms like loyalty, patriotism, considerate, and faithful bid for an effect and have no tangible referents. Terms like disloyal, unpatriotic, inconsiderate, and unfaithful bid for an effect and have no tangible referents. We use many of these operator terms that exist purely for the effect they have on others.

Using general or abstract words guarantees that we talk without tangible reference, but for effect only. Much advertising shows this structure. For example: "Well-bred, sophisticated, with-it people prefer the taste of Upcola. So join the crowd of modern, in-step, genteel Americans and drink America's Upcola."

We spot this negotiation easily. When someone uses the same approach in personal negotiations, we may assume that something more personal is being requested of us.

When people speak with general or abstract words, their statements become unclear. The wife whose husband complains that she doesn't love him cannot know what he wants. The abstract word "love" does not point to anything tangible. Unless someone helps this husband learn how to talk, he will never solve the problem between him and his wife. General or abstract words thwart many of our attempts to say something to one another. *Then our wish to understand tempts us to resort to interpersonal habit. We may discontent to try to gain our wish to be understood.* Out goes any view of peace.

General or abstract words affect others. We keep them for their utility. We do not keep them to reference something because they do not reference anything. They operate, and so we use them to operate. Trying to understand with them is futile.

We can see that our language structure subserves interpersonal habit when we notice how people talk. Frequently the speaker describes himself as either object or not identifiable. For example, we say "You made me angry." This describes the self as an object. We say, "Everybody likes honey." This describes the self as not identified. This structure conceals the speaker as subject and keeps him as an object or as anonymous. An infant enjoys the role of being an object or passive or not-yet named. When a speaker describes himself as an object or as unnamed, he assumes the infant role. He structures his language to cast himself in that role. An infant role always entails blindness to one's personal peace. Interpersonal habit takes priority over personal peace.

Contrast these structures with the statement "I'm angry." That structure describes me as a subject acting. We don't usually talk that way. We seldom clearly describe ourselves as subjects acting. That description would clearly take us away from the infant role and open our eyes to viewing our peaceful state.

Many sentences are structured to conceal the active role of the speaker. For example, "I don't know what makes me do that." This sentence nicely conceals the speaker as a subject acting and depicts him as an object. This sentence keeps him in the passive, object, infant role with personal peace well hidden.

Having a *not-I* to use as subject well serves our negotiation strategies. Many variations of the not-I appear as subjects in our sentences: *no one, everyone, people, it,* and *you.* "It makes me sad," for example. Having no I, no person, we can certainly have no personal peace.

Perhaps you have noticed that very small children do not use the term "I." They use the names that others address them by or the object case to refer to themselves. Baby says, "Me wants a cookie." This infant way of talking persists as we grow older. We cling to it and the infant role by using sophisticated not-I terms.

Frequently adults use the word "you" when referring to themselves. "You don't like bigots" often means "I don't like bigots."

This operating without an I contributes nicely to low self-esteeming. Having no I contributes to self-negation. With no I, there can be no peaceful I.

We say many things that have no corresponding form in our physical world. We can talk about *mermaids and unicorns and witches.* These obvious cases keep company with many not so obvious ones, such as *patriotism, love, faith, good,* or *bad.* We use such words to negotiate because they affect others. Having gained an effect, we show little concern for the absence of any *tangible* referent.

These kinds of language use leave the whole business of using words on shaky grounds as far as exchanging information goes. Exchanging words and exchanging information relate only loosely. We can surely spot the operations done with words, and surely spot the interpersonal negotiation. We *cannot* surely know the validity of reference. I can more easily spot what you want your words to get me to do than spot the discernible referent. You need to know this because when your wish for information goes begging, interpersonal habit tempts you by promising wish fulfillment. Out will go your peace.

Knowing that talk frequently supplies no information will allow you to listen without expecting sure information. Then when no information comes, you can remain peaceful. You can pass the temptation to resort to interpersonal habits. You can pass the temptation to use irritation, discontenting, or angering to try to gain your wish for information.

7

Let's Talk About Feelings

I must teach you what happens when we talk about feelings because most often talking about feelings involves abandoning personal peace.

We often say the word *feelings* when we talk with each other. A child learns to say, "I feel this" or "I feel that" because these words affect others. He says that he feels afraid, and his parents move to comfort him. His parents' responses reinforce his use of the words "I feel."

The noun *feeling* and the verb *feel* are metaphors. The terms derive from the literal acts of touching and feeling something with our fingers or with other body areas. We employ the metaphor to allude to some supposed experience inside our skin.

Operationally, we say "I feel" to affect others. We commonly negotiate by saying "I feel." Since we learn to negotiate in this way very early in life, before we could make our words stand for things, this method is a deeply rooted component of our interpersonal habit. Interpersonal habit predicts that we will receive reinforcing responses from the other when we say "I feel."

When we negotiate by saying "I feel," we complete the sentence with an object to produce the effect. We say, "I feel *something*." We say, "I feel bad" or "I feel good." We say, "I feel sad" or "I feel happy." We say, "I feel angry" or "I feel pleased." We so use the words *afraid, anxious, calm, hurt,* or *joyful.* We so use *dissatisfied, satisfied, helpless,* or *weak.* We report that we feel confident, guilty, right, or ashamed. We report that we feel embarrased, hurt, hungry, or thirsty. We say that we feel cold, hot, upset, worried, or comforted. *Most often when we practice the habit of reporting feelings we have lost sight of our personal peace.*

We can group these reported feelings into the three general categories of *discontent, satisfaction,* and *pleasure.* These three categories are enough, even though we grow more capable and our words become more sophisticated. And we do create artful contents for the form "I feel whatever." "I can't feel anything" provides a sophisticated content for "I feel discontent." But the sophistication brings no personal peace.

Consider the three reported feelings of *anxiety, guilt,* and *anger.* A man reports feeling anxious, guilty, or angry. We can only observe the report. The report supposedly refers to some experiential event that he has had, but we cannot get inside his skin to know of this experience. We can only accept that he experiences some event known only to himself.

He describes the event as discontent. He doesn't like it. He admits of no peace.

I will agree that people have "feelings," but I cannot observe these feelings. I can see and hear people *report feelings.* Significantly, I know that we can reinforce this behavior. Dr. Skinner's principle of operant conditioning applies. We can reinforce the behavior of reporting feelings just as we can reinforce any other behavior.

A child receives more or less reinforcing responses from parents when he reports different feelings. These responses shape his interpersonal habit: he learns which feelings get results in which situations. He learns that talking about his feelings can be a powerful negotiating technique. In some situations, he learns that reporting anxiety will succeed. In other situations, guilt or anger will achieve a better response.

A child's primary negotiating strategy may be taken from any one of the three general categories of discontent, satisfaction, or pleasure. But most parental responses in early infancy relate to crying or other behaviors associated with discontent. And as the child grows, his parents still respond more readily to signs of discontent. Children get more reinforcement for reporting anxiety, guilt, anger, unhappiness, or hurt. And so reporting these feelings becomes an overriding dictate of their interpersonal habit.

Later in adult life this habit appears as a dependency on reporting discontent as a position for negotiation or a bid for care from others. *Almost all adults show a dependency upon reporting or displaying discontent as a way to negotiate.* So almost all avoid any sighting of their peaceful state.

We see adults arrange and maintain their discontent in hundreds of creative ways. Much of the way we talk bears on the need to maintain an image of discontent. We say, "Work kills." We say, "Being idle is boring." We say, "The world is in terrible condition." We say, "Thank God, it's Friday," and "Oh no, not chicken again." Every area of our lives furnishes us with a hundred more examples.

A person conditioned to report and show discontent as a dominant way of negotiating experiences life as discontent. Do the fishes see the sea? The person who depends on anxiety sees and experiences a fearful world. The person who depends on guilt sees and experiences an accusing and judging world. The person who depends on anger sees and experiences a blame-worthy world. The person who depends on sadness sees and experiences a sorrowful world. None of these can see or experience any of the peace and comfort that surrounds them.

Of all the ways that parents reinforce their children's earliest behavior, the reinforcement of feeling behaviors is the strongest influence on a person's experience of the world and of life. Each of us *learns* our own particular way of perceiving and experiencing life. We *learn* to perceive and experience a life void of personal peace.

Since we learn these ways of seeing and experiencing, we may also learn to transcend them. I want to teach you that these reported feelings *of discontent* are all merely attempts to negotiate. Discontent is not our state, but rather our doing. I want you to learn that you create your perceptions of discontent. All the while, your state remains one of peace and comfort. You merely throw that awareness of peace away in your habit of reporting discontent. Talking about your discontent bids for others to do your wishes but does not remove your state of peace. I want to give you a new experience that will teach you new ways of viewing how you report your feelings and release you from your dependency on discontent. I want to give you an experience of the personal peace that remains behind the smoke screen of discontent.

You can begin by practicing two exercises. The next time you are with someone and you think that your companion is experiencing some feeling, invite him to describe it. Invite him by using a sentence that starts with "I." For example, "I wish you would share that feeling with me. When you feel something, I wish you would share it with me."

If your companion does report a feeling, you can take a further step. Tell your companion, "I would like to know what it is you wish I would do when I discover that you feel angry." If your companion can tell you what they wish, things will become very clear between you. Once your companion has specified the wish underlying the feeling, you can decide what to do.

Then the two of you can decide whether the wish is possible or practical and whether you want to fulfill it. For example, your companion may say that she feels dissatisfied because she wishes that you would fix something besides ham and eggs when it is your turn to cook. You probably could grant that wish. Talking her feelings through to the wish behind it will help clarify and improve your relationship. If your companion feels helpless and decides that this is so because he wishes to be a baby again, you can both see that this is a nice but impossible wish.

Your companions will not always be able to say what they wish you would do in response to their reported feelings. But sooner or later, some of the time, they will be able to say what they wish. Gradually you will clarify many things in your relationships.

As a second exercise, watch for the next time that you experience a feeling. Take this feeling as a clue that you are working on something that you wish for from your companion. Say to yourself, "I am feeling discontented. I am wishing for something from my companion." You can usually expect yourself to be wishing for tangible things like a wish that he would hold you. Or a wish that he would let you do some of the driving. You may even wish that he would say what *he* wishes.

Once you have taken the feeling as a clue to a wish, and have discovered your wish, ask for the wish. If the wish is practical and possible, the other will usually do it. Even if the wish is impossible, asking for it will help clarify your relationship.

If it is important to your companion *not* to gratify your wish, you benefit from finding that out. Finding this out will help you assess your relationship. When you clarify many such issues, and discover that many of your wishes go unhonored, then you learn something very important about your relationship. (You may learn that you wish to end it.) Conversely, clarifying your wishes gives your companion the opportunity to honor more of your wishes. When this happens, you benefit by learning to cherish your relationship.

I want you to start practicing these two exercises

regularly. Invite your companion to report his feelings and search for the wishes he works on with the feelings he reports. Use your own feelings as clues that you are working on wishes of your own. Search for these wishes and ask for them.

Be sure to start all your sentences with "I." Since you want your companion to be clear about his wishes, it's essential for you to be clear about your own. Using "I sentences will keep your intentions out in the open and go a long way toward clarifying just who is asking for what.

I promise that these exercises will help you to clarify your relationships and to expend less effort on them. With regular practice, you will become skillful at interpreting your feelings and identifying the specific wishes behind them. When you ask for what you wish and succeed, you achieve fulfillment. When your wish goes unmet, you still gain some very important benefits.

First, you'll learn that an unmet wish isn't really a very terrible thing. When we bid and negotiate through discontent, we keep our wishes hidden from ourselves. And so we never really look at what we want or experience it for what it is. And how hard is it to give up a wish? Will your unmet wishes cut you until you bleed? Will they crush you until you bruise? You'll soon find out that *you can forgo wishes without bleeding or bruising or impairing your personal peace.*

Your wishes have something else to teach you as well. More often than not, behind the stiff mask of discontent, you'll uncover a quiet, unthreatening, and very human wish—a longing to be hugged, or comforted, or talked to, or noticed, or praised. With discontent, you talk yourself into perceiving a hostile, malevolent world thrusting its dissatisfaction upon you. *Your wishes show you no such world.* By interpreting your anxiety or guilt or anger or sadness as an unmet wish for comfort, you turn your attention to that wish. You turn your attention away from a malevolent and fearsome world. You perceive your unmet wish, rather than an accusinjg and judging world. You turn your attention away from a blameworthy and delinquent world. You perceive your unmet wishes, rather than a haunted, sorrow-filled world.

Knowing *that* you wish and *what* you wish for will give you the opportunity to ask for what you wish. Often you will succeed and achieve fulfillment. Discovering that you do not bleed or bruise from your unmet wishes will give you the confidence to forgo them. In time, your habit of discontenting as a bid for fulfillment will lose its vigor. Your view of your personal peace will grow more steadfast.

8

Old Forms with New Contents

We plunge into the world of interpersonal operations equipped with only a few forms of operating. We use the forms of operating that succeeded in infancy and childhood. As we age, capacities for intellectual prowess increase. We employ this expanded intellectual capability to create new contents for these old dependable forms. *The content of our operations changes as we age, but the forms do not change.*

We exercise our capacity for referential speech to make statements and convey images to affect the other. Our sophisticated statements merely serve up our old dependable operations with cosmetic content. All our complaints about our spouse merely serve up the old infant whining form. We duly expect this image to effect some comforting response from our companion of the moment.

By looking for the form it takes and keeping our attention on the here-and-now we may see and read the interpersonal operation. We may transcend our blindness. We may see the interpersonal world.

The newborn infant cries. He thus exercises a potent operation on Mother to effect the sweetest experience. Mother responds. She picks him up and cuddles

nurses him at the breast. His suffering operation succeeds, and he receives abundant reinforcement for it. His
suffering operation becomes a solidly established tool in
his interpersonal habit.

Crying displays the appearance of suffering. Crying
becomes the prototype of variations such as sadding,
hurting, or guilting. Sadding, hurting, and guilting like-
wise display the appearance of suffering. They too
become tools in the child's interpersonal habit.

For most of us, in our here-and-now everyday life,
pain is an infrequent occurrence. But the infant does not
hesitate to use his often successful crying operation. He
cries to negotiate with pain or without pain. Later he
becomes proficient with whining and whimpering. Whining and whimpering display the appearance of suffering
and frequently succeed in gaining maternal response.

As he grows older and more capable he learns to sad.
Sadding displays the appearance of suffering. He can sad
with facial expression and posture. When he gains
speech, he can report sadding by asserting that he *feels*
sad. No one can get inside his body to dispute his asser-
tion. His sadding operation frequently succeeds in evok-
ing a comforting maternal response.

We can sad as surely as we can lift an arm. We use
the power of our words to create a sad mood. We get out
all of our sad thoughts. We can tell ourselves about lost
times, lost pets, and lost friends. We can tell ourselves
about lost lovers, lost ambitions, and lost hopes and
dreams. We can tell ourselves about lost parents and lost
babies. We can boost ourself straightaway into sadding
with our self-talk. Then we can use our sadding to operate on those around us. Our interpersonal habit says that
our sadding will achieve a comforting response from
them.

I see thinking as talking to oneself not out loud. The
word *thinking* points to our habit of talking to ourself
(or *self-talking*). Our words and our self-talk skills ena-

ble us to maintain an atmosphere of sac
images. We can report our sad words
operate with others for their comforting
interpersonal habit directs such action. P
remains unseen.

Our ability to enter the world of words ... us
from the here and now. Using words, we can self-talk
about sad other times and sad other places. We can self-
talk about lost and starving people. We can self-talk about
warring and abused peoples. We can self-talk about dis-
eased and plagued peoples. All of these images maintain
the atmosphere of discontent that our interpersonal
habit calls for.

The media diligently serves our requirement for bad
news and sad news. And there is a ready market for the
deluge of bad news that the media sells us. The majority
of people spend a large part of their day glued to news-
print or an electronic screen. Perhaps we tire of doing all
our discontenting on our own with our self-talk. That
requires effort. The media feeds us our sadding while we
sit passive. The ideal mother brings things to us. We
prefer spoonfeeding to foraging. Having garnered the
day's bad news, we can proceed to operate on each other
with it. We can present our discontent to our friends
with the full expectation of a supportive response.

Most persons create and maintain an ambience of
sadness from an early age. They pursue this operation
with such constancy that they do not know that they
create their illusion of a sad world. They have no way to
know that they create what they see. As far as they know,
their sad world is a sad fact. They fully gain their interpersonal habit before they have the capacity to talk about
what they do.

We employ the suffering form when we negotiate by
reporting that we feel hurt. We use many variations of
this content. The metaphor of *hurt feelings* serves well as
content for this form. Few will question our use of the

aphor as a literal fact. Most will respond with the comforting concession we expect. We report hurt feelings when our companion does not do what we wish. We impute an image of brutality to our companion who must then do what we wish to avoid such an appearance. Doing what we wish approximates the maternal comfort that our hurting evoked in infancy.

Reporting hurt feelings works well when both parties subscribe to the system. And most of us commonly do. Almost all of us use this bid since almost all of us experience success with it in childhood. "You hurt me" routinely evokes response from the other person. Few ever question the hurt. This method can admit to no personal peace.

Sally says, "I better call home, else Mother will worry." Mother has convinced Sally that without some exact response by Sally worry will attack Mother. Worry equates with suffering. Replacing the word *worry* with the word *suffer* clarifies the form that Sally's mother is using. We use worrying as a sophisticated content for our old reliable form of suffering.

Some of us frequently report feelings of guilt. Mother taught us well by her nurturing responses when we guilted. Now we frequently say, "I'm sorry." To add force we say, "I am so sorry," or "I am terribly ashamed." Guilt parades in all this as a painful experience. Few question the existence of suffering. We do not question these interpersonal operations since the whole system developed before we could talk and question.

Before I can guilt regularly, I must regularly engage in behaviors about which I can say, "I'm sorry." Any behavior that affects the other will do. With some all I have to do is hold my fork wrong. With others who are harder to affect I may have to rob a bank. With most, the kind of behavior I can guilt about lies somewhere between these two extremes. In every case, we design the content to fit the other's unique vulnerabilities. The form remains our old reliable suffering. Interpersonal habit says that suffering by guilting will get a comforting response.

In all these old habits for negotiating for our wishes from others we concentrate on forms of discontenting. This concentration entails remaining blind to our true state of personal peace. We attend to discontenting and don't attend to our peaceful state.

9

Third Person Camouflages

Jack rails on and on about his inconsiderate wife. He pours forth his hostility in detailed images of her many transgressions. To unexamined appearances, his hostility is aimed at his wife. But whom does he actually hostile with? *He hostiles with his companion of the moment.* He operates with his here-and-now companion.

We conduct all our interpersonal operations with the other who is with us here and now. When we cast the operation to involve a third person, this camouflage obscures the immediate, intimate, and personal target. The companion seldom sees that the operator negotiates with him. The companion seldom takes issue with or objects to such negotiations.

You can learn to see through operations framed in third-person terms. You can learn to identify the real target of this especially misleading technique.

This technique supplies an abundance of content for all forms of interpersonal operation. Media reports about the world provide us with images of an abundance of third persons. We can anger toward these third persons in the presence of our friends. We can pity them or suffer for them. We can sad for them or inferior about them. We can bombard our friends with such talk. Our friends receive our angering, pitying, suffering, or sadding. Our talk operates on them.

We can arrange our lives to involve an abundance of third persons. We can hostile, dissatisfy, or sad about these third persons with our friends. We can tell our friends these others abuse us or victimize us. We can present ourselves as superior to them or we can worship them with our friends. Our friends will probably not recognize that we are operating on them and not on the third parties.

We can reach to the past for third persons such as mother, father, brother, or child abuser. We can report about these. We can present our here-and-now companion with whatever images fit our operation of the moment. Our operation can present images of ourselves helplessing, inferioring, or victiming with father. We can present our friend images of ourselves being deprived, sadding, angering, or bragging with mother. We can use reports of teasing or clowning with our brother to operate with our friend.

We can similarly reach into the future for other third persons, such as sons, daughters, suervisors, politicians, or the Russians.

All of these third persons provide us with an abundance of images that we can use to construct our operation of the moment. Future third parties often provide images for fearing, worrying, or suffering. We can fear, worry, and suffer about our daughter's future. We can fear and worry about what the politicians or the Russians may do. We can frustrate, anxiety, anger, or helpless about what our supervisor may do. Then we use these creations to operate with our here-and-now companion.

The here-and-now other may never suspect that *the operation manipulates him and negotiates with him.* Having learned to watch the here-and-now, you can see that it does.

Mr. Citizen usually responds with a reinforcing reflex. He usually assures, sympathizes, or comforts. He frequently joins in with the consensus. And so the nego-tiator frequently finds complementarity and reinforce-ment to perpetuate this style of negotiation. But neither of the two can talk about what they do with each other by way of all these third persons. The whole interaction follows the dictates of interpersonal habit.

As an enlightened people watcher, you know that the present other operates with you. You know that the here-and-now other targets *you* for the reinforcing responses he seeks. You then have three options. You can reinforce his bid by responding to it. Or you can pass on it by just listening. You also have the option to talk to the other about the interpersonal operation you see here and now.

If you choose this last option, you may evoke a storm. Take care! Talking with a slave of interpersonal habit about here-and-now operations will consistently result in an even more vigorous pursuit of the negotia-tion. This subsequent negotiation will follow the dictates of the particular person's interpersonal habit.

For example, if you expose an angering third-person operation, the strategy will shift to a "hurt feeling" oper-ation aimed directly at you. This negotiation can rapidly turn to crying, hostiling, or withdrawing as the other continues to try to achieve his desired response.

Negotiations like these are stormy, fast moving, and tricky. Dealing with a relationship during such times requires a high level of skill. Such skill can only come from experience and good training.

10

Picking a Partner
Complementarity

We choose our friends, lovers, or spouses by a process that serves our and their interpersonal habit. I suggested this when I told you about Tom and Nancy in Chapter One. Not just anyone chooses anyone. Obeying our interpersonal habit, we choose others by spying out a complementary interpersonal habit in them. The rapidity and the accuracy of this choosing process approaches the uncanny.

Mabel married a drunk. When sober, Hank displayed a kind and caring personality, even a groveling and placating one. He did tend to overstate things and showed a facility for exaggeration. When Hank got drunk he abused Mabel with both his words and his fists. Mabel said, "That's not the real Hank, not the Hank I love." Nevertheless, that was the Hank she lived with, since Hank stayed drunk. Hank eventually killed himself in an automobile. Then Mabel married Sam. Sam was also a drunk. The second marriage paralleled the first. After five years, Mabel divorced Sam and married Joe. Joe shortly became a drunk also. So Mabel continues her life arrangement of interpersonal adversity, frequent abuse, and general unhappiness.

What roles does Mabel's interpersonal habit prescribe for her? Her behavior tells us. She requires a partner who can help her remain upset, abused, and abounding in troubles. She requires a partner who can help her remain a victim and a martyr. Her interpersonal habit calls for her to perform those roles in order to negotiate with others. She uses those self-images to effect a supportive response from others.

An interpersonal habit complementary to Mabel's is one that combines ineptitude and blaming hostility. Such a complementary habit would call for helplessing, self-depreciation, and self-damage for successful operating with others.

Mabel infallibly picks a perfect match. She picks a mate with a complementary interpersonal habit time after time.

Mabel's system does work to an extent. Neighbors try to help her for a time. Ministers spend much time counseling her. The whole church prays for her. Acquaintances in her neighborhood regularly discuss her sorry plight. She basks in her infamy. *But Mabel pays a very high price for her elixir.* Does Mabel know about what she arranges? Do the fish see the sea?

We arrive into an interpersonal world and proceed to learn an interpersonal habit. The habit we learned as infants continues to dominate us as we grow. As infants, we were totally dependent on our set of negotiations for sustenance. As we grow older, we cling to our habit with the same total dependency.

Our lives evolve into a constant plying of interpersonal negotiations. We even continue this activity when we are alone. We ply our negotiations in what we tell ourselves. We ply our negotiations in what we tell others. We ply our negotiations in all that we do. The thoughts or fantasies that we entertain are negotiations. The reports that we make to others are negotiations. *Our negotiations dictate how we live our daily lives.*

Our negotiations take first priority, even when they extract a high price for their maintenance. This insight explains why people arange their lives in ways that are harmful to them. Their arrangements often extract a price in discontent and suffering. Their arrangements may extract a price in physical damage and health damage. At times, our negotiations may even extract a price of death.

Interpersonal habit dictates that the negotiation must go on without regard for price. The infant who learned the habit knew nothing of time, and so now the habit is timeless, with no knowledge of the future or of death. Since the habit knows no literal death, dying can only be another interpersonal operation. Dying can be used to negotiate, just like hurting or suffering or running away.

Now we can see why Mabel lives the life she lives. Her interpersonal habit chooses an inept and abusing husband for her. Without this husband, she could not maintain the self-image that her interpersonal habit demands—the self-image of an abused, victimized, and unhappy child. She could not maintain her self-image of a struggling child drowning in problems.

As a child, those images were successful—she obtained her mother's milk and her mother's care. Now she negotiates by using those same images to gain attention, comfort and companionship from those around her.

Those who gather around her pursue their own complementary interpersonal habits. As children, those others learned that helping, parenting, and performing would succeed with mother. Now their interpersonal habits tell them that suffering with Mabel will bring them mother's attention and praise.

Mabel's cohorts also pay a high price to pursue their own brand of interpersonal habit. Mabel requires much of their time. She may even require their money. Even though they make heroic attempts, their remedies never work. Mabel's life arrangements remain entrenched. Any momentary shadows of comfort that her friends provide prove fleeting.

Mabel and each of her would-be helpers have

erected a stable system which subserves the interpersonal habit of both. For both, interpersonal habit maneuvers them into the path ordained as the way to mother's milk. Each does exactly what formerly succeeded. And all interpersonal relationships of more than momentary duration show this complementarity. The complementarity of both interpersonal habits fashions the choreography of the relationship. Personal peace also never enters into such arrangements.

No two relationships waltz the same waltz. Since each person practices a unique interpersonal habit, any two habits will complement each other in a unique way. Nevertheless, many similarities abound, and so we can easily spot the particulars of any relationship.

The price paid by the pair in a relationship varies from very mild to fatal. Some complementary pairs extract little sweat, blood, and tears. Others extract much. Some relationships tax little, while some tax voraciously. When you have learned to see your own ways of negotiating, you can then assess the price you are paying. You can spot when you give up seeing your personal peace.

A high price may so obscure the underlying wish fulfillment in a relationship that both partners strongly deny experiencing any fulfillment at all. Similarly, a child may deny the good taste of his ice cream cone. But when he continues to eat it, we hold his report suspect. So denied fulfillment in a continuing relationship stands suspect.

I do not doubt that such complementary pairs remain blind to whatever wish fulfillment lives in the relationship. Storms and troubles are highly dramatic, and the habit systems that we forged as children are far from visible. We learned those habits before we could speak, and now we do not speak about them. We report neither the negotiation nor the rewards.

Do the fish see the sea, or report it? Do we talk about our *interpersonal world* or report what we do to negotiate it? Not ordinarily.

11

Life Arrangements as Interpersonal Operation

Maggie lived a continually miserable life. Husband Herman criticized her to the point of verbal abuse, punctuated by occasional brutal hostility. He demanded, remonstrated, and managed to maintain an irrevocable position of complete dissatisfaction with her. He maintained total control over the family money, requiring her to ask for any she needed to spend.

The architecture of Maggie's marriage had become apparent within the first year and had persisted throughout twelve years since. Maggie had suspended her education part way through college to marry and so she had no means of earning a living and no vocation. This factor contributed to the stability of the miserable relationship. The two had managed to bear four children, which provided a further reason for continuing the marriage. Maggie's children required her care, and so she was confirmed in her rationale that she could not change anything about her life.

Such arrangements don't just happen. This sordid relationship, which extracted a high price in misery, conformed to Maggie's interpersonal habit. What strategies worked with Maggie's mother? You might guess that unhappying and appearing abused succeeded. You might guess that fearing and helplessing succeeded. You might guess that distressing, sadding, and despairing succeeded in getting a nurturing response from her otherwise inattentive mother.

How do I know about Maggie? I sat as therapist with her for several years. I had the honor and privilege of carefully examining how she operated in an interpersonal dyad. I could easily spot her negotiations with me, those same operations which must have succeeded with her mother. She negotiated by unhappying and reporting abuse. She operated by fearing and helplessing with me. She operated by distressing and sadding with me. She finally operated with me by despairing.

She *unhappied* by recounting at length each week's spousal abuse and hostility. She *helplessed* by discounting the viability for any plan to better things for herself. She *distressed* about the behavior of her children. She *feared* that I would abandon her. She *despaired* of any mitigation of her misery.

Maggie displayed her set of characteristic operations right before my eyes and into my ears. Her life arrangements ratified these operations. Her life gave her an environment exactly suited to her particular set of negotiations.

Marrying an abusive man allowed her to negotiate from the abused position. In other words, she arranged her life to accommodate her set of negotiations. That fact showed that the arrangements she had made were themselves negotiations, and in her accustomed forms. *Our life arrangements negotiate our interpersonal world.*

Maggie and I sat together regularly, negotiating with each other. I mostly listened, but occasionally would invite her to watch how she operated with me. Little changed for a long time. Eventually, she began to concede the possibility that she did operate with me. She admitted that her helplessing might bid for me to help. She began to talk about her operations with me and mine with her. We examined each negotiation in her set as it occurred between us right there in the room.

Maggie learned to spot her operations. She learned to talk about them and to report them.

Meanwhile she changed nothing in her life. The climax came when she despaired over this lack of change. She sat with me and negotiated wholeheartedly with her despair. And then she spotted the negotiation. She talked at length with me about this most miserable of her negotiations.

With no dramatic accompaniments, she began to systematically rearrange her life. She finished her education over Herman's objections and belittlement. She landed an excellent job, which made her financially independent. She divorced Herman.

She then began to operate with me with performance. She reported her successes. She operated with peacefuling and joying. She reported the gratifications of her job. She reported enjoying the fellowship of her co-workers. She operated by helping and parenting. She reported how she helped her children and people she met at work. She moved into new living accommodations closer to her work place. In substance, she rearranged her life. She made arrangements which ratified her new way of negotiating the interpersonal world. She was able to confess her personal peace.

I admire Maggie. She invested much time and effort in her pursuit of therapy, and she taught me a lot. She taught me to watch for a rearrangement in a person's life as a necessary indication of improvement. I use the term *improvement* here to describe what happens when we arrange to negotiate the interpersonal environment at a lesser price. It also describes what happens when we arrange to negotiate the interpersonal environment with some peace, joy, and tranquility.

I have shared Maggie with you to demonstrate that life arrangements are negotiations. After years of similar experiences, I know that this principle applies to us all.

You can watch and identify anyone's interpersonal habit. That habit's set of behaviors displays itself in what others tell themselves. It displays itself in what they report. It displays itself in what they say and what they do. Their interpersonal habit and its dictated behaviors display themselves in *how they arrange their life*.

A facile people watcher sees these life arrangement operations. They go on within the view of everyone. You can learn to see these continual operations. You can learn to spot them and discuss them. *Nothing is hidden.*

Do the fishes see the sea? Maggie learned to see her interpersonal world and she achieved some mastery over it.

As we survey society, we see the masses living joyless to utterly miserable lives. All of these lives are arranged as interpersonal operations, according to an interpersonal habit that dictates various forms of misery as paths to success. When we grasp that misery formerly succeeded and that we retain that habit, we begin to grasp the architecture of human misery. You can see that people live in an unattended state of peace and comfort while *they do their misery*.

That architecture appalls us at first sight. At first sight we deny or discount what we have seen. Yet only by squarely looking and seeing can we manage to perceive some alternatives.

I belong to a sophisticated study group. Almost to a person, the interpersonal operations I witness in it rest upon some form of discontenting. The members of the group all prosper economically, and few suffer true health problems. Yet the statements they continually make to each other strongly agree that "the world is in bad shape." They operate by talking about bad news. They deal with each other by ruminating at length upon distant problems. Practically never does anyone point out some boon.

Though well-to-do, well-educated, and intelligent, they remain slaves to an oppressive interpersonal habit. They remain slaves to an oppressive interpersonal habit that they do not even suspect exists. And when you get to know the particulars of this group's life arrangements, you discover that those arrangements subserve the same oppressive interpersonal habit.

Their life arrangements subserve a habit that calls for continual discontenting. Divorces abound. Several suffer alcohol dependency. They frequently engage in self-depreciation. They report all manner of family problems. Do they see their interpersonal world? Do the fishes see the sea? The tragedy of not seeing extracts a very high price.

Sam dropped out of high school and entered the army. Being of high intelligence, he did well with machinery. He married a young woman, Minnie, who had also dropped out of school and had no vocation. Minnie thus arranged an obligatory dependence on Sam. He fathered two children with Minnie. Having to care for the children enhanced her dependence upon him.

Sam provided minimum necessities for his family. He spent all his spare time and much of his earnings souping up his auto. Risk taking became a noticeable facet of his daily life. The streets he drove became undeclared raceways. The inevitable happened. He misjudged when passing a car in traffic and crashed, breaking his back. Sam became paraplegic from the waist down.

The army medically retired Sam and he assumed the life of a semi-invalid. In spite of much rehabilitation, including vocational training, Sam perceived himself as totally disabled. He complained of much pain for which the physicians could find no definitive basis. This pain loomed larger in his interpersonal bids when physicians gave analgesics. He negotiated with hostility toward anyone who tried to help. He accused his helpers of malevolence. He blamed them and subjected them to vituperation. He negotiated continually by reporting pain.

Sam had arranged his life so he could negotiate according to his interpersonal habit. That habit called for angering, attacking, and suffering.

What parades as an accident is no accident at all. We see an artfully executed arrangement. Sam and his family pay a high price to arrange and practice his interpersonal habit. Does Sam see that he arranged his life? Do the fishes see the sea?

You can see that any of several forms of discontenting can become the chief currencies of interpersonal habits. Tobacco and alcohol stand ready to assist in arranging a discontented life. Tobacco dependence works by undermining health and promoting sicking. Secondarily, tobacco dependence supports weaking, suffering, and helplessing.

Alcohol dependency undermines health and family relations. Alcohol dependency impairs one's ability to work and one's social relations. It provides an efficient route to inepting and helplessing and a prime support for sicking and guilting. It supports badding or criminaling, from petty to homicidal. When one's interpersonal habit dictates those behaviors as paths to success with mother, alcohol dependency provides the means.

As a small child, bright young Adam learned early to succeed with mother by reversing roles and taking care of her. He learned to comfort her and to do good. Once, when she caught him exploring under the skirts of a five-year-old playmate, his mother responded with what looked like a convulsion. From incidents like this, he learned to do whatever she wished in order to avoid her dissolving into tears or collapsing in a hysterical faint. Good boy Adam did well in school. He did housework. He patted mother on the hand and did anything to placate her.

In fact, her fragiling frightened him, but he learned to appear strong. He learned to avoid displaying his fear and thus avoid mother's further discomforting.

Adam studied surgery after completing medical school. He conducts a vigorous practice and takes good care of his patients. His choice of medicine as a profession does not surprise us. He already knows how to take care of the weak and fragile. He moves into familiar territory.

Adam carries significant handicaps. He only knows how to negotiate with others by playing parent. That position makes it against the rules for him to admit ignorance. Not admitting he doesn't know makes it difficult for him to learn and accept teaching. His brightness carries him through and he completes his courses, carefully avoiding self-exposure as much as possible.

Adam, the surgeon, does with others just what he has done since childhood. He takes care of them like he took care of mother.

Adam picks a wife. What kind of woman does he know how to deal with? A woman who negotiates by weaking, helplessing, fragiling, distressing, and collapsing. Adam's experience enables him to spot the perfect wife with facility. During courtship he treats her nicely and caringly and she appreciates him so. She just melts in his arms.

Come marriage and the honeymoon is over. The more Adam helps and comforts, the more his wife helplesses, inepts, and distresses. Adam spends more and more time working, thereby cutting down the time he has to face his unhappy wife. On occasion he resorts to a strategy that worked when he was too small to take care of mother. He hostiles with his wife and verbally abuses her. He reprimands her for her ineptitude. She responds with crying and cringing.

Her physician pronounces her depressed. She and Adam continue to live in the same house, but keep their contact down to a matter of seconds per day. Adam lives for his patients, and his wife becomes an interminable psychiatric patient.

Interpersonal habit has had its way. This couple with affluent resources live lives of slavish work and overworked misery. What comes next? A divorce, to start the whole system again with someone else?

People can do only what they know to do. Interpersonally, they follow the system that succeeded so well during life's beginning. As long as they cannot report their system, they cannot see it. They remain slaves to their unseen system despite its oppressive price.

All infants try operating on mother with angering. At an early age mother responds by giving her milk. We all succeed to some extent with angering and hostiling. As we grow in size and capacities, we develop the creativity to use sophisticated content for our hostiling. Further success with angering assures that angering will remain a practice in our set of interpersonal negotiations.

Interpersonal habit regards angering and raging as dependable, almost fail-safe negotiations. Thus we readily agree that raging and killing will obtain whatever we ordain as the path to mother's milk. Most of us readily agree to *war*. We readily agree to the proper killing of the proper people at the proper time. We easily convince people that war and killing will succeed since their interpersonal habits also affirm that raging gets mother's milk.

War on the largest scale simply arranges life to suit our common interpersonal habit. As in the case of other interpersonal operations, war also disregards the price. Like other operations, war depends on the illusion that the here-and-now world remains a mother-infant world. The habit and the illusion say that rage has succeeded in the past and that rage will still succeed. Personal peace remains unseen and unconfessed.

No wonder, as the often quoted phrase has it, "There will always be wars and rumors of wars."

12

Society Maintains an Ambience of Discontenting

So far I have taught you that we first succeed with mother chiefly by using discontenting. Occasionally we get to mother by quieting or by happying. But when these strategies fail, we count on discontenting. Every person undergoes this same process of learning to operate with mother as an infant. Everyone starts life with the same equipment. So everyone in society ends up with an interpersonal habit that relies on discontenting to do the trick.

Since all of its members embrace this same habit, society reflects that habit by zealously displaying an ambience of discontenting.

The media conspicuously parade this ambience. News broadcasts and newspapers concern themselves almost exclusively with tragic events, or the probabilities of tragic events. To be news it must be bad news. Editors seldom deviate from this pattern. The public desires food for its habit of discontenting. The public will buy and pay for such food. The media literally scan the earth to find tragedy to feed their viewers and readers.

We depend on the word world to surround ourselves with the tragic. With words we bring in the sorrows and troubles that we lack in our here and now. We import material for discontenting just like we import any valuable commodity. We import to supply our requirement for assistance in our discontenting.

We bestow social esteem on "keeping up" with current events. *Keeping up* means a constant feeding upon bad news. Keeping up does not mean keeping informed concerning *all* events

What sells as entertainment provides us tragedy. For entertainment, we buy suspense and violence. For entertainment, we buy scenes of interpersonal animosity, conflict, and danger. For entertainment, we buy scenes of crime, injustice, and cruelty. These reports and scenes help us create our discontenting. We dignify the enterprise by calling it entertainment. Few notice that the ten-second happy ending only serves as an excuse for the two hours we spent suffering our esteemed discontenting.

In the work world of factory or business, morale requires constant attention. *Interpersonal operations always take priority over the conduct of business.* While their work waits, the clerks whimper to each other about how they suffer neglect at home. Secretaries tell stories about their children's problems, keeping themselves and co-workers tied up while the work waits. Supervisors whine to their secretaries about inept wives, and the work waits. When managers aren't trading complaints, they function chiefly to keep the business moving in spite of these handicaps.

Committees notoriously drag inefficiently. Any sharp people watcher can spot that interpersonal operations take priority over the conduct of business. The show-off shows off, the hostiler hostiles, the complainer complains, and the joker jokes. The pessimist despairs, the dissatisfier finds wrongs. The committee scarcely considers its charge to study and recommend. With everybody contributing, we can effectively keep the workplace discontented. Seldom does any eccentric pop up to pronounce the workplace a place of joy. Thank God it's Friday.

The politician practices his stock technique. He emphasizes public discontenting. He promises to absolve that discontenting. Even if he were sincere, gnats can't move bulldozers. The analogy fits his situation.

Since the public relishes blaming, it subscribes to this game. By electing the promising politician, we get to blame him. He then earns his pay trying to juggle all of his constituents' unhappiness. Seldom does he manage to placate anyone. Nevertheless, he dutifully passes the complaints to some supposedly appropriate government agency. That agency can't make the individual happy either. Mr. Taxpayer gets soaked. Of course, the soaking provides him with an excuse for discontenting for the day or for the year.

We meet an acquaintance at the grocery store. Immediately, she begins to tell us all her bad news. Her husband had to change jobs and her part-time employer dropped her after many years of working for him.

This type of interaction largely characterizes social meetings. Talk of unpleasant things dominates the agenda. Gatherings of people adeptly maintain a consensus that our world presents us with great difficulties. They agree that the world struggles and chokes with problems. We all stick together to help each other create and maintain that discontenting on which we so depend. "Pass the gravy, please."

The moral of this chapter is that you can count on society to help you discontent and remain blind to your state of personal peace.

13

Let's Look at Personal Histories

Once I suffered a drug reaction and landed in a medical intensive care unit. I lay for several days with wires and tubes attached, monitored. Thus anchored to my bed, I entertained myself by listening and people watching.

One midnight, a man arrived on the unit after he attempted suicide by drinking isopropyl alcohol. His nurse took a history from him. He candidly pictured himself as a person who had overcome the adversities of a humble beginning. He portrayed himself emerging as a war hero. His report contradicted his present state. His observable state displayed him as an alcohol-dependent streetperson struck down by self-neglect.

The next day this man gave a history to the consultant psychiatrist, a male physician. This time he candidly pictured himself as victim of those around him. He described himself as deprived and abused. He portrayed himself as cheated and unfairly treated. He pictured himself as kept down by a hostile society.

This incident illustrates how our personally reported histories subserve interpersonal operations. We construct the history we report by selecting from thousands of events. From those events we create a content that fits the operation we are using at the moment. When our man operated by presenting a performing image, his history depicted that image. When he operated by presenting the image of a misused waif, his history displayed that image.

We construct our personal histories to operate interpersonally. We say whatever interpersonal habit says will succeed. We portray ourselves however that habit prescribes. We picture ourselves as hero or abused waif according to the dictates of interpersonal habit. We say what we want the other to hear.

Accordingly, the degree of veracity of a personal history report varies from some to none. This could pose a problem to a psychotherapist or a people watcher. It does pose a problem for therapists who depend on personal histories as a path to know their clients.

As skilled people watcher, you can watch the operation in the here and now. You can grasp the form of the operation. The content of what is said does not divert you. You can see all the person's past parade forth in his operations in the here-and-now. The operations our subject uses succeeded in his distant past. The operations our subject uses reveal everything of significance about his past.

As a skilled people watcher, you can see the subject's past much more clearly than the subject does himself. The operations he uses now reflect his real past. Without some new enlightenment, the subject cannot report his significant past. Without some new enlightenment, the subject cannot know about or report the events that had real significance for his interpersonal world.

Often when two witnesses report the same event their reports differ substantially. Their reports may even contradict each other. Again we find the problem that reports of any sort subserve the person's interpersonal operation. Each witness's particular style of negotiating biases his report. Interpersonal operation takes priority over strictly factual reporting. The notion of objectivity is simply an illusion.

And the truth? The truth is only what interpersonal habit knows as truth. Whatever operations worked in the dawning interpersonal world become the truth. One witness reports to portray himself as astute, performing, and infallible. Another witness reports to portray himself as bungling, inept, and helplessing.

This problem pervades all reports by us humans. Interpersonal operations take first priority over the presentation of merely observed facts. By watching the here-and-now interpersonal operations, you can see this process going on.

14

More Hints to People Watchers

Action happens here and now. Only words refer to past and future. Action lives now, so we can spot interpersonal operations only here and now. Getting sidetracked into listening to your self-talk blocks you from watching what you and I do with each other. Listening to self-talk blocks us from watching the operations we do with each other. Learning to keep our gaze on the here-and-now requires regular practice.

When you try to watch operations, one big factor can interfere. You cannot watch someone else's negotiation and do your own operation at the same time. When you begin operating, your own operation will take priority. Your own operation will distract your attention and supplant your attempt to watch the negotiation.

You may find yourself beginning to frame his operation as good or bad, right or wrong, foolish or wise. You have begun to operate by *judging*. Your judgment follows from your own wishes about how you want the other to operate. *Good*, *right*, or *wise* means that you wish him to continue his operation. *Bad*, *wrong*, or *foolish* means that you wish him to operate differently. Once begun, your judging operation will divert you from any disinterested observation. Your own action becomes a pursuit of wishes. Your own action diverts your gaze from his operation.

You must choose between observing his operation and doing your own. You cannot do both since one excludes the other. This same interference happens whether you begin to judge his operation or your own. Any attribution of good and evil makes people watching impossible.

Certain starting premises prove fruitful for people watching. We can adopt the premise that this person is the perfect and only example of herself. She provides the only source from which we can ever know her set of operations and her style.

I can know her perfect example only by watching while *not trying to change her*. I can know her only by watching while not trying to make her into something else of my own pleasing.

A profound paradox shows here. I can see a person *only when I give her up*. I see her operations only when I can let her operate her way. I can see her operations only when I forgo any wishes I might have about the way she operates.

When two people continually work at changing each other, neither ever sees the other. Neither sees the unvarnished other. They see only a fantasied image. They never see the unspoiled perfect example.

The premise that she is perfect helps make it clear that my saying otherwise only speaks of my own unmet wishes toward her. When I pronounce her imperfect I speak of myself and not of her. I speak of my own unmet wishes toward her and not about her.

You have already learned many other premises. It all happens here and now. The negotiations continue every moment, watched or not. Avoid getting blinded by content. Watch for the simple forms. Entertain the view, "What does this action bid for me to do now?" Simplicity characterizes all interpersonal negotiations, so keep your eye out for the simple. No matter how sophisticated the content, sadding bids for comforting. Whining bids for holding. Helplessing bids for your picking me up. Angering bids for feeding. All those operations bid for picking up, holding, cuddling, and feeding. All bid for mother's milk. All such doings hide the state of peace.

Our people-watching skills take a leap forward when we learn that we exercise limited wisdom. Our limited wisdom cannot know how another should operate. Our limited wisdom cannot know how the world should be. Recognizing our limited wisdom frees us to observe and learn. Recognizing our limited wisdom frees us to observe without having to make things right.

As a disinterested observer, you will see the negotiations that people do without attaching any more or less value to any one of them. The cool people watcher has no preference as to what operation the person uses to pursue her wishes. The cool people watcher just wants to identify the operation form, whatever that operation may be.

Since all interpersonal operations pursue interpersonal wishes, no particular operation has a different intrinsic value than any other. Crying, sadding, helplessing, suffering, angering, performing, happying, or asking all have the same intrinsic value. One way to work on a wish is as good as any other. The outcome depends on how the other person negotiates. One way may work and another may not. This reflects only circumstance and says nothing for or against the value of the operation.

Once you accept that a person has to work on her wishes some way, you can watch and learn the way she works. If you fight against how she plies her wishes, you will rob yourself of the chance to see and learn. Learning how she plies her wishes shows you clearly what used to work when she began her interpersonal journey. You can see her past and know how her life proceeded before age five. Those who try to shape how she negotiates can never get to know her. Most people do just that. Trying to change the other partly accounts for most people's blindness about interpersonal negotiation.

Trying to help blocks our seeing the other person's

negotiations. Proceeding on the assumption that she needs help casts her down into an infant role. The assumption that I can help casts me up into a parent role. When I try to help, I immediately engage in a parenting operation. If I am busy parenting, then I cannot be a cool people watcher. I cannot see her for trying to fix her. I sink into the negotiation. I cannot assume a detached perch and just watch and see how she proceeds.

Watching and listening will make your people watching work. Talking can block your seeing. Talking can turn into an operation of your own and plunge you into the negotiation. This spoils your chance for disinterested observation. Talking spoils your chance to see and know how the other person operates.

An occasional expression of interest will not block. Explanations and teachings will block. Advice giving will block. Comforting and reassuring will block because with them we do our own operation. When we speak in these blocking ways, we abandon our project to watch and see. We talk and begin an operation of our own.

Your people-watching skill will get a boost when you assume that whatever a person does, she does in self-interest. A person's actions may appear otherwise to an outsider. Nevertheless, with every action or nonaction she takes she pursues self-interest. Her experiences say that the action she takes will further her self-interest. Our experience may say otherwise. But her interpersonal habit defines what action will benefit her. An outsider does not know her interpersonal habit and operates from his own. From the view at the center of her world, everything she does will work in her interest.

Embracing this assumption entails my adopting the view that I always act in self-interest also. I act in self-interest as far as my experiences say the act will further my interest.

Proceeding from this assumption simplifies people watching. Acknowledging self-interest helps you see through tricky statements such as "He puts everyone's interest above his own." The person who appears to live for others does so because his interpersonal habit dictates that image from which to negotiate. His habit says that the image of the faithful servant will serve his self-interest.

The person who tries to persuade you to live for others tries to persuade you to devote yourself to him. He belongs to that group of others whom he suggests you serve. He blatantly pursues self-interest. Such tricky statements do not mislead a skilled people watcher. The form shines through the content. Nothing is hidden.

Most people live without a here-and-now. They have a past. They have a body of reports about their past. They use these reports as content for their interpersonal negotiations. "I grew up during the depression." "My mother never took good care of me." "I was an Eagle Scout."

Similarly, they have a future. They entertain a set of thoughts about the future. They use these thoughts as content for interpersonal negotiations. "I fear my children may get cancer." "This government will get to us one way or another." "Tomorrow I will discover the secret of liking myself." "Getting a new wife will solve my problems." "Having some children will make our marriage work."

This constant eye on the past or future becomes the continual preoccupation of the common man. The past and future exist only in words and words are most convenient for doing interpersonal habit. Common man has *no present*. He has no here-and-now, the only place he could grasp his peaceful state.

Common man uncommonly experiences the smell of the flowers or the beauty of the sunset. Common man uncommonly experiences the warmth of an embrace or the sensual ecstasy of a sexual meeting. Common man uncommonly experiences the nicety of a waltz or the warmth of hand in hand sharing the path. All these exist only here and now. Common man's eye remains glued to the past and the future. This bondage robs him of now's delights. This bondage keeps him from seeing his personal peace.

15

Enlightenment

I want the gift of enlightenment for you. When you see your own personal peace and see that others exist in a peaceful state, you approach enlightenment. When you see how we do our misery and throw away our sight of peace, you have stepped toward enlightenment. When you see that your judgments of good or bad only mirror your own wishes, you have taken another step. When you spot your interpersonal habits and know them as bids for wishes, you have taken another step. When you see your bids for wishes with disinterest and forgo your wishes without throwing away your tranquility, you approach enlightenment. When you see others as perfect examples of themselves, when you can watch and enjoy without trying to change, you take another step. When you so firmly grasp your personal peace that you pronounce the world perfect, you have achieved enlightenment.

The possibility for such a miracle slumbers latently in each adult-with-adult relationship. Adults carry certain capacities which come with their emergence from infant-childhood. These capacities blossom by age thirteen. The adult has these capacities though he may seldom or never employ them. These capacities make possible a happy escape from the tyranny of interpersonal habit.

Things are possible for two people that are impossible for one. The obvious example of making babies serves as a good analogy for this class of events. Things can happen within an interpersonal relationship that cannot happen with a person alone. The power of relationship coupled with adult capacities creates the possibility of that splendid escape from slavery to interpersonal habit.

Adults can employ referential speech. They can learn to identify interpersonal operations, which the infant-child could not do. Nevertheless, they can only identify what they can see. Only from within a relationship can you experience the interpersonal negotiations here and now. In the negotiation's momentary existence you can experience it and know it.

A living relationship provides the only laboratory for seeing interpersonal negotiations. A living relationship provides the only laboratory for experiencing and knowing interpersonal operations.

We can talk about only that which we know. In relationship with you, I can watch and spot how you operate. In relationship with you, I can watch how you bid. In relationship with you I can watch how you negotiate. In relationship with me, you can watch and spot how I operate. There you can watch how I bid and how I negotiate. Once experienced, we can employ our adult capacity to *talk about* these negotiations.

Similarly, as we relate you can watch and spot your own negotiations. You have the possibility to learn about yourself. You can then talk about and think about your own set of interpersonal operations. You can learn to see how you manage your own interpersonal world. When you see what you do, you may devise some alternatives. You may figure out how to negotiate for your wishes more effectively and at a lower cost.

A relationship between adults can serve as a laboratory where each learns to see their own interpersonal methods. This splendid event in a relationship can happen naturally though experience and training help.

You must devote time and effort to the enterprise. You must spend time regularly and continue your studies of the relationship for an extended period. This type of investment can make it possible for the enlightenment potential of the relationship to blossom.

It takes nine months to make a baby. It takes time and practice to achieve a rebirth into freedom from the slavery of interpersonal habit.

The capacity for referential speech brings the capacity to say what I wish. The infant-child can work on his wishes only with behavior. He can work on his wishes only by doing whatever interpersonal habit dictates. He may work with feeling behaviors such as sadding or badding. He may work by reporting for effect. He may say, "My teacher hates me." Interpersonal habit says that you already know my wishes. Interpersonal habit says I need not tell you my wishes.

You have the capacity to recognize your separateness. You have the capacity to recognize that you probably do not know what I wish. You can use this capacity to see separateness. You can recognize that you know my wishes only when I tell them. You could not do these things while you remained slave to interpersonal habit. You have the capacity for enlightenment. You can tell me what you wish.

You have the capacity to feed yourself and to provide for yourself. I can say no to your spoken wishes without harming you. The infant works for life-sustaining nurture. Mother cannot say no. As adults we can say "I wish," and the other can say yes or no to our wishes.

Saying what I wish keeps things perfectly clear. Saying what I wish simplifies our negotiations. Saying what we wish assures that whatever we do together we do by mutual desire. Saying what we wish keeps things clear. Saying yes or no to each other's spoken wishes avoids any slavery. By reporting our wishes and accepting yes or no, we each maintain our freedom within our relationship. We honor each other's unique self.

You have the capacity to forgo your wishes. You can

say "I wish" to self or others but not act further. You can forgo working on the wish with behaviors or with feelings. You can forgo engaging in further negotiations for the wish. You can forgo throwing away your peace.

The infant-child cannot forgo. He keeps working on a wish by using this operation and that operation. He works until he hits upon some operation that succeeds or else exhausts himself.

The adult's capacity to forgo makes "no" a comfortable and easy part of an enlightened adult relationship. When we can say no to each other's wishes without further bother, our relationship proceeds smoothly. I certainly want you to be able to say no to my wishes. Otherwise I could never know when you really said yes. Submission takes away both no and yes. I prefer a friend to a slave.

Yes and no cannot be a part of the mother-infant structure or its tyrannical interpersonal habit. Once an adult pair learn the value of being able to say no, their relationship becomes much less arduous.

Your ability to forgo wishes makes possible an equal-to-equal relationship. You and I do only what we mutually agree to do. We honor each other's separateness. We treasure each other's individuality and protect it. We negotiate with spoken wishes. We can say yes or no to each other. We share the path together, each doing a unique but complementary pattern.

A waltz portrays a suitable analogy for this equal relationship. The waltz depends on each doing a different but complementary part. It depends on separateness and individual uniqueness.

Your ability to forgo wishes allows you to let me do things my way. Your ability to forgo frees you to not respond to my negotiations. Your abilty to forgo frees you to enjoy my presence. My ability to forgo allows me to do the same with you.

Stripped of the illusions of interpersonal habit, you can recognize my presence as my most precious and most abiding gift. You can then begin to see *your pres-*

ence as your own most precious and most abiding gift to me.

Once seen, this knowledge of the value of presence brings peace and ease to the relationship. Knowing the value of your own presence removes any need for you to perform or to please. Knowing the value of your presence removes any need to apologize or to make amends. You know that you already do more than enough when you share your presence with me.

Interpersonal habit dictates exclusiveness for relationships and has no place for third parties. The adult ability to forgo wishes allows you to abandon this demand for exclusiveness. You can allow your friends to have relationships with others. You can enjoy your friends having relationships with others. You can like to see your friends enjoy other people. You want enjoyment for your friends, and this includes enjoyment from others.

This capacity to abandon the demand for exclusiveness looms important between husband and wife with the appearance of a new baby. The husband can enjoy the separate and unique relationship between mother and baby. The wife can enjoy the separate and unique relationship between husband and baby.

When the demand for exclusiveness prevails, the coming of a new baby presents the new family with insurmountable problems. The circumstances make exclusiveness impossible. The spouses cannot grant each other's wish for exclusiveness. Spouses resort to all the discontenting which interpersonal habit dictates will bring fulfillment of any wish. The family becomes a cauldron of unpleasantry. All sight of peace disappears. The old methods which succeeded in mother-infant circumstances remain impotent to fulfill impossible wishes. The old habit traps the family in a mire of difficulty.

Spouses who have transcended interpersonal habit forgo the wish for exclusiveness. They can enjoy each other's enjoyment of a relationship with baby. Each day family life proceeds with ease and comfort.

Your adult ability to forgo wishes enables you to realize that you have no needs. You have wishes, but no needs. You may say, "But you need food to survive." My reply is: "I don't need to survive." I wish to survive. I enjoy survival as a luxury and a gift. I do not need to survive.

Any fulfillment of a wish provides only luxury and not need. Dumping the illusion of needs will make your interpersonal life easy and comfortable. Wishes fulfilled provide luxury. Wishes unfulfilled represent no loss. When we can fulfill our friends, we and they experience luxury. When we cannot, we nor they experience loss.

Your friend may still live under the mastery of interpersonal habit. He may see your not fulfilling him as a loss and a travesty. As an adult, you know that you can trust your eyes and ears. You can see that he doesn't bleed, or fall ill, or die. You know that saying no to his requests does him no harm. You can take his whining or angering as merely his way of working on his wishes. You can allow him that without giving up your peace or your esteem for the value of his presence.

As an adult, you have the ability to distinguish the content of interpersonal operations from the form. When the portly businessman grumbles about his steak, you can grasp that he whines. He does a simple infant operation which formerly succeeded. The sophistication of the words and the circumstances does not fool you. You can see that the man pursues a simple wish in his infantlike way. You can accept the negotiation and treasure the man's presence.

Adulthood brings the ability to forgo wishes and the ability to accept refusal of our requests. It is interesting that these adult capacities arrive about the time that sexual capacity arrives. Using those abilities, adults can relate sexually as equals when they have learned to relate as equals in other ways. But adults in sexual relationships may remain trapped in interpersonal habit, and carry in all the burdens of slavery to that habit. Such adults perform many troublesome interpersonal operations to attempt to fulfill their sexual wishes. Interpersonal habits prevent sexual pleasure and peace.

Your adult capacity to forgo wishes enables you to abandon the notions of good and evil. You can see that I call good what I wish. You can see that I call bad what I wish not. You can spot the interpersonal operation that this notion of good and evil serves. You can see that I bid for what I wish by labeling it good. You can see that I bid against what I don't wish by calling it bad. That seeing enables you to dump the illusion of some universal good and evil. You escape the "knowledge of good and evil." You escape that burdensome illusion.

You can realize that one who uses the notion of good and evil merely displays their own wishes. You can then respond to those wishes with yes or no or no response at all. You can respond as you would with any other wish. The tyranny of good and evil vanishes with the vanishing of the illusion. You do not have to watch for these rules any more. You will experience more unburdening. More peace and more ease will pervade your relationships.

You will discover that we do and share only what both agree to do and share. You may discover that each treasures and protects the separateness and uniqueness of the other. You will discover that each does a different but complementary part. You may discover that each gives our most precious gift by giving our presence. You will see we create a unique, mutual, and unfolding relationship. You may discover that this relationship has no obligations and no responsibilities except those agreed upon by both.

The relationship, like a path, continually changes and continually brings new experiences. Released from the slavery of interpersonal habit, the relationship flows easily and peacefully. The relationship proceeds comfortably and bestows much gratification while extracting a very small price.

16

Let's Talk About Psychotherapy

Have you ever worked wth a coach or trainer? The same operations that occur in a coaching situation also apply in psychotherapy. The essentials of psychotherapy consist of regular meetings at a regular place. The participants meet at a regular time and meet for an agreed time for each session. They continue their meetings over a long period.

Athletic or physical training takes time, regularity, persistence and concentration. So does therapy. Athletic training can enable you to transcend your physical limits. Therapy can enable you to transcend the tyranny of interpersonal habit.

Incredibly, almost everyone tells himself that he can do therapy. Ignorance cannot know of itself. Sometimes people read a book about psychotherapy and then tell themselves that they have the ability to act as therapists. Those calling themselves therapists come in all varieties. They come from many professions or from no profession at all. Each entertains his own theories about therapy. Each likes his own theories about therapy best. Most of these theories merely serve up interpersonal habit in sophisticated clothing.

Some hold to a popular theory that therapy consists

of *reparenting* the client. They tell themselves that they must provide good parenting for this unfortunate who had such woeful parents. This theory merely displays a sophisticated content for the operation of *hostiling with parents*. In this case, as in many others, the aspiring therapist's operation with his aspiring student directly reflects the therapist's interpersonal habit. His operation shows that interpersonal habit yet enslaves this aspiring therapist.

Therapies primarily grounded in some theory of pathology—that is, based on the notion that the client is sick—do not enable escape from interpersonal habit. Any such benefits occur incidentally, almost in spite of the therapy. And some benefit can occur incidentally from *any* intimate relationship, since we humans do inherently gain from each other's presence.

Sometimes proponents of a therapy or therapist proclaim success when patients report that the experience gratified them. They cannot know what they have not experienced. They cannot know there can be more to therapy than momentary gratification.

For the past hundred years, psychology has assumed some causative agent as the basis for human tribulations. In contrast, I assume that *I do my life*. Contemporary psychology assumes that bad parents cause human tribulation. Or it assumes that bad environment or traumatic events or bad thoughts cause human discontent.

These agents look to me exactly like new contents for all the ancient superstititions about evil spirits, possession by devils, bad air, or sinfulness. All represent various contents for what I described before as *not-I* or *something outside myself as the doer of my life*.

These theories hamper any chances of escape from the tyranny of interpersonal habit. They hamper chances of escape by focusing your study away from *your* here-and-now behavior. They focus your study away from your here-and-now life arrangements, and away from what you say here and now about your past and your feelings. They focus your attention away from all your here-and-now negotiations.

Theories of this kind are typical of the illusions about therapy that psychotherapists commonly entertain. Most theories by which would-be therapists conduct their therapies merely serve up interpersonal habit in sophisticated content. I do not judge or blame such therapists. The unenlightened cannot know that they do not know enlightenment. Ignorance cannot know of its own existence.

Therapy at its best offers the apprentice a chance to escape the tyranny of interpersonal habit. Since everyone begins life as slave to interpersonal habit, anyone can use such an opportunity. That makes us all candidates. Some interpersonal habits extract higher prices than others. Those carrying the burden of an expensive habit may seem to require therapy more than the less burdened. Nevertheless, anyone who achieves that splendid escape will have a more peaceful, easier, and less arduous life.

The best therapist is the one who has mastered the skill of seeing interpersonal negotiations. I call such a person a master. But anyone calling himself a therapist must first escape the slavery of interpersonal habit. Otherwise the so-called therapy can only proceed as the blind attempting to lead the blind.

Formal training may or may not so equip the aspiring therapist. Excellent training programs produce only a few masters. Excellent training programs produce only a few therapists capable of providing the liberating experience that all of us seek.

The whole arena of therapeutic endeavor depends upon art, not science. Both the master and the apprentice must have a talent for this art of liberation and enlightenment. Life does not deal fairly with people. Some have the gift of talent and some do not. With the talented apprentice, a master can invite the apprentice to look in the appropriate places at the appropriate time. The gifted apprentice will see and learn to read the interpersonal negotiations that the master calls to his attention.

Successful therapy proceeds in steps. The master invites attention to the operations that the apprentice does in relation to the master. The master points up the operations at the very instant the apprentice operates. Gradually the apprentice begins to see how he works with the master. Gradually the apprentice begins to see how he pursues his wishes. He begins to see that he operates by sadding, whimpering, and helplessing. He begins to see that he operates by suffering, inferioring, and performing. He begins to see that he negotiates by afraiding and angering. Gradually, he begins reporting his operations. He learns to recognize what wishes they work for.

Eventually, he reports and talks about what he wishes. He talks about how he works on those wishes. He also learns to see and read the master's operations. He learns to recognize what wishes the master pursues and how he pursues them. Nothing is hidden.

When the apprentice learns to talk about what he wishes, he gains a new view. When the apprentice can talk about how he works on his wishes, he gains a view which offers alternatives. His ability to forgo wishes enables him to work on wishes and accept that the master leaves them unfulfilled. He can accept the master's saying no to his expressed wishes.

Recognizing all of his wishes toward the master enables the apprentice to distinguish those that the master fulfills and those that the master does not. This process clarifies the basis of their relationship. He discovers that his *presence* provides the chief and reliable gratification that the master gains from their relationship. He discovers that the master's *presence* provides his own chief and reliable gratification in the relationship. This discovery unburdens the relationship from all the tyranny of bids and wishes and leaves some room for peace and comfort in the here-and-now.

Metaphorically put, master and apprentice feed on each other's presence. This cannot happen as long as either tries to fix or change the other. This cannot happen as long as either tries to help or cure the other. Such attempts immediately cast the relation into the parent-infant mold, and the tyranny of interpersonal habit takes over.

Therapy proceeds by watching the negotiations that take place in the here-and-now. Therapy proceeds by learning to read those negotiations. The pair talk about the negotiations that occur and learn to report the wishes pursued in these negotiations. The pair forgo many of these wishes, learning that they can forgo them without harm. The pair learn to treasure both yes and no responses.

They learn to sit together without trying to change each other. They abandon trying to fix each other. The pair learn to see and know the nurture of each other's presence. They learn to forgo all their unmet wishes in the relationship without effort. Having given up working on unmet wishes, they can see the many *fulfilled* wishes in the relationship.

The pair recognize the many fulfilled wishes which, at first, they had obscured by their constant working on unmet wishes. Under the tyranny of interpersonal habit, the relationship had appeared totally unfulfilled. Their preoccupation with a few unmet wishes had overshadowed all the fulfillments. But now they can see that the relationship is almost entirely fulfilled.

When the master does not do the apprentice's expressed wishes, the apprentice learns to put his wishes in a benign perspective. He sees that he does not bleed or fall ill or die in the face of the master's no. He begins to realize that interpersonal habit dictates wishes and not needs. He realizes that interpersonal habit dictates wishes that he can forgo without harm. He experiences an unburdening of all needs. He can abandon any notion of need. He can see that his fulfilled wishes are luxuries and his unfulfilled wishes are no loss.

The apprentice recognizes that all his former discontenting merely pursued his wishes. Now he gains release from that dependence on discontenting. He can allow his true state of peace and comfort to come to view and to prevail. He finds new subjects to talk about, and sad news no longer dominates what he says.

The apprentice can also begin to change the discontenting life arrangements which his interpersonal habit formerly dictated to him. He can give up the constant self-depreciation which interpersonal habit dictated as imperative. He can begin to confess that he has value to himself and others. He can confess that giving others his presence gives them his most precious gift.

He can make friends with all of his wishes. Since he knows that any wish can be forgone, he also knows that no one wish can reign over his life with its tyrannical demands. He knows that no wish is dangerous. He recognizes his mastery over all his wishes, and so he gets over his caution about wishing. Any wish that seems unworkable he merely forgoes. Mastering his wishes, he gains liberation from the wish-slavery of his interpersonal habit.

Strangely, most persons have difficulty making friends with their wish that someone hold and nurse them with a mother's milk. You may have noticed that many persons cannot accept the care offered by another. Few can confess that they wish for someone to baby them.

The enlightened confess their wish that someone baby them, hold them, and nurse them with a mother's milk. At the same moment an adult admits that wish, he also gives it up. The time for such fulfillment has past. (Does this wish make you feel uncomfortable? What wish does this discomfort pursue, if not the very wish denied?) The enlightened can be joyful in the face of his impossible wish to nurse. He can value himself for the humanity this wish displays. He can turn with joy to the timely fulfillments in the nurture of the other's presence.

For many years many professionals have held the theory that sexual wishes form the basis of people's intranquility. Viewed in this way, sexual wishes and sexual activities can make up the content for guilting and inferioring. Sexual matters can make up the content for badding and hostiling. Sexual matters can make up the content for suffering and afraiding. Sexual matters can make up the content for any operation that an interpersonal habit requires.

We would all rather experience problems with our sophisticated, grownup sexual wishes than to experience problems with our unsophisticated baby wishes. The therapies we turn to reflect that preference, and much therapeutic effort goes toward trying to unravel sexual problems which supposedly cause the apprentice's unhappy life.

In therapy, we find that sex merely veils the fundamental problems. Behind the sophisticated content, we find that the apprentice negotiates with operations from his mother-infant relationship. Those operations pursue his wish that someone baby him. Often we see sex used as bargaining currency in negotiations. Each partner wishes to be babied. Sometimes sex is the payment for that wish. Sometimes sex is the sign of its fulfillment, the symbol of the breast milk each negotiates for.

How easily we relegate sex to the status of a bargaining chip! Since we do so, this must mean that sex has a low priority as an end in itself in interpersonal negotiations.

With sexual sharing between equals, sex is shared for sex itself as an end. Equals share sex as a limited pleasure that they can agree to share without deforming it into a means toward other ends.

Biologically, sex chiefly provides simple recreation. The infrequent success in procreating proves that sex serves only secondarily for procreation. In the service of tyrannical interpersonal habits, most people saddle sex with many other functions. This misappropriation of sex robs most people of ease and comfort in their sexuality.

In effective psychotherapy, the apprentice learns to read interpersonal negotiations independently of their content. He learns to avoid misdirection by sexual content. He learns to see his sexuality as a capacity for recreation with an appropriate partner.

Monogamy, though not a necessity, has the advantages of convenience and economy. Monogamy provides the opportunity to learn how to enjoy this other. Monogamy minimizes the chances of contracting sexually transmitted diseases. But the many other social demands and superstitions concerning monogamy merely reflect the rules of interpersonal habit. Interpersonal habit insists on exclusivity in sexual relationships. Exclusivity is simply the structure of the mother-infant experience transferred to all other relationships. The framing of these rules in religious or ethical terms merely serves to properly sophisticate the content.

Recall the steps the apprentice makes. He learns to spot his interpersonal negotiations. He learns to read them, and to talk about them. He learns what wishes he pursues and how he pursues them. He learns to request his wishes with words. He learns to accept yes or no in answer to his requests. He learns to forgo. He learns the value of his presence, and that of the master. He abandons discontenting as his preferred way of negotiating. He learns to spot the large number of wishes that the therapeutic relationship fulfills. He learns to tolerate peace.

He abandons the notion of good and evil. He learns to live in the here-and-now. Having escaped his slavery to perpetual discontenting, he can relax and be peaceful. He knows that *he* does his life. He can smell the flowers, hear the music, enjoy the sunsets. He can receive the nurture of his companion's presence. He can enjoy a waltz. He can taste his good food for the first time.

Who can make that splendid escape?

17

Tricked by a Mirror

When Joe calls something bad or good, he works on his wishes in a form dictated by his interpersonal habit. The child calls his mother bad to get her to do what he wishes. Mother calls the child bad to get him to do what she wishes. When we judge, we merely display our own wishes. Our judging something good or bad displays nothing other than our own wishes.

Our preoccupation with word maps leads us to the illusion that our judgments have some universal validity. When we say "bad world," or "bad politician," or "bad drunk," we tell ourselves that our judgments have universal validity. Actually, we simply display our own wishes about the person or situation that we judge. Confident of our illusions, a mirror tricks us. That mirror of our own unmet wishes tricks us into illusion about persons and situations. We tell ourselves that goodness or badness is a quality of the persons or situations that we judge. But I say that good and bad belong to the one who judges and like a mirror merely reflect his wishes.

The author warned us concerning the knowledge of good and evil in his creation story in Genesis. Perhaps the author of the myth somehow knew that knowledge of good and evil merely mirrors our own unmet wishes. He advised us well to avoid that fruit.

All our pronouncements of approval or disapproval merely display our own wishes. Such pronouncements stand as revelations of ourselves for anyone who reads people to see.

The enlightened man holds this as a treasure because he wishes to see himself clearly. This mirror furthers fulfillment of that wish. The enlightened man has dumped the illusion that his judgments have universal validity. But he still watches for them to further acquaint himself with his own unmet wishes.

Judgments expressed by others will give you knowledge about their unmet wishes. Knowing this, the enlightened man avoids contentions concerning the differing judgments of those around him. He wants each to have his own wishes and to know what those are. He wants to know his fellow man and to enjoy him. He wants to feed on the companionship of his fellow man and does not want to change him.

When a man judges himself, he similarly works on his own unmet wishes about himself. When he believes in his judgments, the mirror has tricked him. His unmet wishes become the mirror that tricks him into illusions about himself.

The operation of self-judgment couples with low self-esteeming. Men commonly assert their imperfections with a confidence beyond any doubt. They uncommonly see that they operate by self-depreciation.

Tricked by a mirror, man blindly judges self and others with confidence. As the Tao masters said, "He lives in the region of good and evil."

18

Peace

Do you hunger this moment? Do you thirst? Do you suffer uncomfortable heat or cold? Does anyone attack you?

I can assume that you have answered no to all these questions, since otherwise you would be busy looking for food, water, or shelter, and not reading this book. So you do experience a state of peace and comfort. Are you aware of that peace in your here-and-now?

Few persons can sit and concentrate on their here-and-now state of peace and comfort. Their interpersonal habit dictates a perpetual discontenting. Faced with peace and comfort, they slavishly begin to entertain all manner of "buts." "But I need to be more attractive." "But I need more money." "But the world's hungry need food." "But the world needs peace." When confronted by their here-and-now peace and comfort, men for the most part quickly return to the self-talk inside their heads. They repeat all the bad news they know, one item after another, until all their talk blots out any view of their comfortable state.

This action demonstrates that they are *not free*. This response demonstrates their slavery to the dictates of interpersonal habit. That habit dictates continual creation and maintenance of discontent. Bad news supplies the outlook to support the illusion that their discontent is well founded.

I want you to suspend your self-talk for a moment. For that moment, I want you to concentrate on your state of peace and comfort. Notice that you do not hunger or thirst. Notice that you suffer no uncomfortable heat or cold. Notice that you suffer no pain. Notice that no one attacks you here and now.

You cannot experience what I am writing about from a book. You can only experience your state in the here-and-now world around you with your five senses. I cannot put your state into words. I want you to look up now from your reading and savor the here-and-now. I want you to leave off your self-talk and sense this state of peace in which you have all along unknowingly existed.

For the most part this state of peace surrounds us all our days. We begin life with indoctrination to the dictatorship of interpersonal habit. The demands of interpersonal habit capture all our attention so that we never see our true state. Enslaved, we perpetually create the discontent dictated by interpersonal habit. We successfully maintain the illusion that discontent is our true state. We remain blind to our state of peace and comfort.

Man is not free but slave to interpersonal habit. Successes in the interpersonal world before age five enslave him.

I assume that you successfully stopped your self-talk. I assume that you gazed around you and savored your here-and-now. I assume that your senses grasped your state of peace and comfort for a moment. Once you sense your state of peace and comfort, your world will never again be the same.

Some really juicy thought useful for discontent may momentarily capture your attention. Nevertheless, your experience of peace and comfort lurks in the background. Your sense of your here-and-now lurks in the background. Your here-and-now awareness says,"I have seen my state and know it is peace and comfort."

Release from slavery to the interpersonal habit enables a new kind of relationship with our others. You know that peace and comfort prevails with them also. This knowledge enables you to watch their negotiations with you with calm. You don't have to rescue others when they come up with some new piece of creative discontent. You know that their negotiations merely pursue their wishes. You know that they can forgo their wishes and come to no harm.

You can watch how they create and maintain their discontent, blind to their state of peace and comfort. You can sit with them and treasure them as persons without any inclination to jump to the rescue. You can sit with them and treasure them without trying to correct their discontent. You can sit with them and treasure them without any compulsion to comfort or to reassure. You can sit with them and treasure them without trying to make things right, since you know that things are already right.

I spoke before of a relationship between equals. I spoke of a relationship with different qualities from the original mother-infant relationship. I spoke of a relationship different from the one in which interpersonal habit arose and became our dictator. A relationship between equals emerges when one of the two has sensed his here-and-now peace and comfort.

Equals relate by stating their wishes with each other. Either can say yes or no to any wish. Whatever they do together, they both agree to do. No obligations or responsibilities enslave, since mutual agreement determines the path of events between them. Nothing forces either. Both remain nondependent, separate, and fully themselves. Neither exercises authority over the other. Neither requires permission or approval from the other. Even the existence of the relationship and its lifetime depend on mutual agreement.

The two meet when they agree to meet, and part when they agree to part. Each retains a separate life apart from the other. The relationship exists only in the here-and-now when they get together. They may picture it or self-talk about it during their time apart. Their moments of verbal and physical intimacy and closeness occur by mutual choice.

These two create a mutual, unique, and unfolding relationship according to the melding of their separate selves. Each holds the other as a privilege and not as a necessity. Neither person wishes nor demands exclusivity. Wanting the companion to be fully self, each expects and treasures that both have relationships with others.

The relationship *has no necessary form* but can shift from form to form by agreement. One can take care of the other. Then the roles can reverse. Or they can share, with neither ministering nor being ministered to. They establish the form of their relationship moment by moment. They show no attachment to any particular form that it takes.

The two may agree to end the relationship. Other contingencies may take priority. In a very cogent sense, *the equals relationship begins with each giving the other up.* The moment a person becomes precious to you is the very moment you face giving them up. As an adult, you know all relationships are temporary. When you recognize the preciousness of the other, you come full face to their impermanence.

Such impermanence finds no place in interpersonal habit. Those who have escaped from interpersonal habit grasp that all relationships are temporary. The adult capacity to forgo wishes enables us to let the other become precious. We know that we will lose that preciousness. We forgo the wish for permanence.

Slaves to interpersonal habit cannot let the other become precious and cannot admit impermanence. When such slaves appear to hold someone precious they merely hold an image precious. They do not hold anyone precious as themselves. They hold precious the image that they hope to negotiate the other into becoming. Those who cannot give up the other can never have the other as he or she is.

Relating as equals involves a continual forgoing of wishes. Our ability to wish far exceeds the ability of any companion to fulfill. And with one we hold precious, wishes abound. Some are impossible, some impractical, and some not according to the inclinations of our other. All these we forgo, since we hold our other's autonomy precious also.

In time the magnetism that attracts equals into relationship turns out to be *wishes that the relationship does fulfill*. The relationship fulfills wishes for presence, for sharing, and for touching. That essential magnetism prevails in spite of many other unmet wishes.

In the struggles of mother-infant structured relationships, the pair overlook or deny the fulfillments of their wishes. They do this to create and maintain the discontent dictated by their interpersonal habits. The pair may admit no fulfillment. Nevertheless, *relationships fulfill many wishes*, whether admitted or not.

Those conducting equals relationships see that their wishes are fulfilled. They see their cup half full and express gratitude. The enlightened see the cup half full even in those relationships that subserve interpersonal habit. The enlightened see some fulfillment when the slaves can see only short shrift and high price.

The high price of relationships that remain slave to interpersonal habit vanishes with equals relationships. The high price of relationships with mother-infant structures vanishes with equals relationships. Equals merely ask and do not suffer in pursuit of their wishes. They do not helpless, inferior, or anger in pursuit of their wishes. They do not live disarranged lives or die in pursuit of their wishes.

When I see how I negotiate for my wishes and what I wish, I can ask for them. I can put them into words. When I say what I wish the other clearly knows what I wish. I pay a small price to ask for and work for my wishes. My clarity allows the other to clearly respond with yes or no. The negotiations of the equals relationship are efficient ones. The partners can focus on doing what they want to do with each other and spend minimal energy and time negotiating.

Personal peace and relating as equals go together. Both come as gifts accompanying enlightenment. Other gifts come in the same package. With enlightenment comes freedom to allow others to become precious. With enlightenment comes freedom from the burden of having to judge others. With enlightenment comes freedom from the illusion that all the world is awry. With enlightenment comes freedom from attachments to particulars. With enlightenment comes freedom from the illusion of need. With enlightenment comes freedom from perpetual searching for that fantasied person or situation which will absolve all of our unmet wishes.

19

The Candle Experience

When a thief meets a thief they require no introduction. When a Buddha meets a Buddha they recognize each other on sight. I have some criteria by which I know that a person has had the candle experience. I call enlightenment the candle experience since the candle has symbolized enlightenment since ancient times.

The enlightened have a here-and-now. They see life as here and now. They have shed the burden of a future and a past. Concerning the future, they do not live dependent on hope. They do not live waiting for some propitious event to bring them life, peace, and joy. They do not daily pay the price. They do not daily spend their resources creating the discontent they suppose will bring mother back to meet their unmet wishes.

Concerning the past, they say, "I live my life." They have dumped the view that not-I, in all its variants, lives their lives. They have dropped the view that not-I things account for their discontent. Past events as not-I disappear from their viewpoint. They do not attribute their state to past circumstances.

They forgive their parents. They confess that whatever their parents were, they were the source of being for them. They reflect gratitude toward their parents as source of their here-and-now with its peace and comfort and occasional joy.

They have cast off the burden of judging others. They have shed the burden of judging the world. Grasping the peace and comfort of here and now, they have shed the burden of any need for understanding. Similarly, they have cast off any burden of needing knowledge. Knowledge becomes merely a pleasure for them to enjoy when convenient. Knowledge no longer looms as an illusory promise of absolution of unmet wishes.

Even survival becomes a mere luxury for them to enjoy and receive with gratitude. They have cast off the burden of viewing survival as a must. They view unmet wishes as one views a swirl of autumn leaves. They quaff fulfilled wishes shamelessly with eyes wide open. They experience every drop and nuance of fulfilled wishes with gratitude.

They quickly see others as precious. They quickly seize the opportunity to create a relationship. They do not quibble at the impermanence of the relationship.

They systematically rearrange their life. They dismantle arrangements that they had designed to image themselves as suffering. They undo arrangements formerly designed to portray them as abused, victimized, or helpless. They abandon arrangements formerly designed to portray them as inferior, needy, or heroic.

They look to others for companionship, relationship, and its fulfillment of wishes. They do not look to others for rescuing, helping, or protecting. They do not look to others for approval, admiration, or judgments. They do not look to others to show them the way.

They do not talk about their problems. Instead they say, "Come walk with me. I just saw a rose, come look with me. Come waltz with me. Let's go look at the sunset. Have a bite of my peanut butter sandwich. Let's go take a shower together. Please hold me. Come sit with me while I die."